Praise for
THIS THREAD OF GOLD

"Catherine Joy White is an extraordinary writer, the kind who turns nonfiction into poetry. Her book *This Thread of Gold* reveals beautifully how the legacy of Black women's writing across generations has woven itself into her heart and soul, and the power of their legacies. It's a stunning debut from a young author, and yet feels, and reads, like it has been decades in the making."

—Afua Hirsch, author of the *Sunday Times* bestseller *Brit(ish)*

"White is not only an incredible writer but a much-needed voice in our current cultural landscape. *This Thread of Gold* shines a spotlight on previously untold stories with grace and nuance—I couldn't put it down."

—Ione Gamble, author of *Poor Little Sick Girls*

"From the moment I heard about this book, I was dying to read it, and when I got a hold of it, I could not put it down. The passion of White's words is infectious. I was constantly fascinated and moved by the way she interwove the stories of the Black women who came before her with her own experiences. I know this book will find many loving readers and I am very excited for them all."   —Okechukwu Nzelu, author of *Here Again Now*

"The stories White weaves are enchanting and inspiring. To be held by her words is an absolute pleasure."

—Ruby Rare, author of *Sex Ed*

"Utterly captivating from the first sentence, this celebration of Black womanhood, joy, and resistance celebrates revolutionary women from across time and space."

—Laura Bates, author of *Men Who Hate Women*

"Monumental. A refusal to back down to an oppressive, reductive version of history. It's even more radical to do this with a tone of pure unadulterated joy; smiling rather than screaming in the face of those who would try and whitewash a rich, beautiful, and momentous tapestry. Kill your masters one symphony at a time."

—Nima Taleghani, actor and writer

"This book is a poetic journey through Black womanhood. It is beautiful. And fragile. And worth its weight in gold. More, actually."

—Parker Sawyers, actor

"In her astonishing celebration of Black womanhood, Catherine Joy White celebrates life itself. Her debut book vividly unleashes the stories of little-known, remarkable Black women, and we hear their voices crackle off the pages as if they are being channeled through her. Reading this book makes you want to be a part of a future which lengthens the thread of gold, making it last forever."

—Angus Imrie, actor

"A poetic meditation on womanhood. A blending of the personal with the political, the magical with reality, and contemporary thinking with ancient stories."

—Rhea Norwood, actor

THIS
THREAD
OF
GOLD

THIS
THREAD
OF
GOLD

A Celebration of Black Womanhood

Catherine Joy White

An imprint of Penguin Random House LLC
penguinrandomhouse.com

First published in hardcover in Great Britain by Dialogue Books, an imprint of
Hachette UK, London, in 2023.

LIBRARY OF CONGRESS CATALOGING-IN-PUBLICATION DATA
Names: White, Catherine Joy, author.
Title: This thread of gold: a celebration of Black womanhood / Catherine Joy White.
Description: New York: Tiny Reparations Books, [2024] |
Includes bibliographical references and index.
Identifiers: LCCN 2023050142 (print) | LCCN 2023050143 (ebook) |
ISBN 9780593475164 (hardcover) | ISBN 9780593475171 (ebook)
Subjects: LCSH: Women, Black—History.
Classification: LCC HQ1163.W45 2024 (print) |
LCC HQ1163 (ebook) | DDC 305.48/896—dc23/eng/20240110
LC record available at https://lccn.loc.gov/2023050142
LC ebook record available at https://lccn.loc.gov/2023050143

Printed in the United States of America
1st Printing

BOOK DESIGN BY DANIEL BROUNT

CONTENTS

To my daughter . . . who saw in me what I considered a scar and redefined it as a world.

—ALICE WALKER, *IN SEARCH OF OUR MOTHERS' GARDENS*[1]

For the sisters & the sistas & the sistahs & the sistren & the women & the womxn & the wimmin & the womyn . . .

—BERNARDINE EVARISTO, *GIRL, WOMAN, OTHER*[2]

For grandmother, mother, and daughter. For you and me; for us. They are in each of us. They are us and we are them. We are this thread of gold.

—CATHERINE JOY WHITE

THIS
THREAD
OF
GOLD

Prologue

CALL OF THE TIDE

A S THE LAST FROST of winter thaws each year and the
first blossoms of spring turn to face the sun, an elderly
Italian woman called Chiara Vigo slips out of her house as
dusk falls. With the Italian coast guard watching over her, she
clothes herself in white, cries out a prayer in a language that
is part ancient Sardinian dialect and part Hebrew. Her words
crash against the rocks in time with the sea's own call as it
brings sand to shore and back out again. And then, Vigo dives
down into the sea of the island of Sant'Antioco, just off from
Sardinia. With nothing but the light of the moon guiding her
way she dives down and up and back down again. Down,
down, and down she dives until eventually she reaches her
destination: a collection of underwater lagoons and caves that
only the women in her family know about. They have known
about them for the past twenty-four generations. It is their

secret. It belongs only to womankind. Still holding her breath as she enters the underwater coves, Chiara Vigo gently and ever so carefully approaches a rare clam known as the *Pinna nobilis*. Measuring three feet tall, this clam secures itself to the bed of the sea with hundreds of minuscule fibers known as "byssus." Chiara Vigo approaches and uses the tiniest of scalpels to gently cut the fibers that grow out of its shell. Delicacy is key in order to preserve the fragile surrounding habitat. She extracts each fiber, leaving the root intact—unharmed—and brings them back up to the surface. Then she cleans them and spins them into finest gold—eventually becoming what we know today as sea silk.

Taught how to dive by her grandmother at the age of three, Vigo is now the only woman left in the world who spins silk from the sea into a thread of gold, but the tradition has a rich and proud history. The fiber was harvested to make robes for King Solomon, woven into bracelets for Nefertiti, and used to adorn the vestments of high priests, popes, and pharaohs. According to Vigo, who is Jewish, the skill of weaving sea silk was brought to Sant'Antioco by Princess Beatrice, the great-granddaughter of biblical figure King Herod the Great. Women passed down their knowledge in the years that followed and some even tried to set up businesses, making money from the sea silk's shine. But no matter how laudable their proposition, their plans always failed. Sudden bankruptcy. Ill health. Byssus was not to be harvested for profit. And so, for more than a thousand years since then, byssus has been woven and spun by generations of women who protect its secret, by Chiara Vigo's ancestors. They passed it down to their daughters, who passed it down to their daughters. It can never be sold, for this is part of its rich woven history. Selling it, Chiara Vigo said in a conversation with the BBC, would be "like trying to profit from the sun or the tides"—impossible. She is bound by a sacred "Sea Oath" that byssus, her own precious sea silk, can never be bought or sold. Instead, these generations of women connected by a thread weave the secret that their mothers taught them into the lives of their daughters, before the daughters in turn eventually hand over the mantle to the next generation: the nieces and the granddaughters whose turn it now is to spin gold.

I was introduced to Chiara Vigo by my friend Kitty Macfarlane, a singer-songwriter whose beautifully crafted song "Sea Silk" explores Vigo's precious legacy.[1] "My grandmother wove in me a tapestry that was impossible to unwind," Vigo said. "Since then, I've dedicated my life to the sea, just as those who have come before me." Like Vigo, I feel unable to remove myself from the women who came before me. I am formed by them. I place my own feet in the prints left by their steps. Their tapestry is woven in me.

In the late 1800s, on the other side of the Atlantic, Harriet Powers, a freedwoman who was born enslaved in Georgia, was weaving and spinning gold of her own. Using the techniques and storytelling often found in the textiles of western Africa, passed down to her from her mother and other

African-American women, Harriet Powers learned the art of appliqué quilt making. In 1886 she made her "Bible Quilt," rich in its narrative, infused with her own personality, and telling Powers's favorite Bible stories. It caught the eye of Jennie Smith, a white artist and teacher who tracked Powers down, desperate to buy it. But Harriet Powers refused. It was not for sale at any price.

Years later, however, at the instigation of her husband in a period of desperate financial hardship, Powers (who had kept in touch with Smith) offered to sell her beloved quilt for a price of ten dollars. Smith was going through difficulties of her own and offered five. Powers hesitated, but her husband insisted, and the deal was made. Powers's quilt was sold. Then, Harriet Powers did the unexpected. In a glorious reclamation of her work, ensuring that it would forever remain a part of her, she painstakingly described to Smith all eleven blocks of its 229 separate pieces of fabric stitched together.[2] Smith wrote the descriptions down, and they live on. Woven into their fabric, so too does Powers's strength—as a woman and as an artist—as does her deep religious faith. Powers's quilts told stories. They were narratives woven from her own experiences and brought to life by age-old crafts and skills she had learned from her ancestors. For her, quilt making was not just an art form, it was a resistance. It was a *reclamation* of what was rightfully hers, a *re-creation* of the story of her life, and a *resilience* to the difficulties she faced. It points to the extraordinary tenacity of Black women to survive over hundreds of years in the face of hardship. It points to their ability to weave the salty waters of the sea into silk of the finest gold.

Not quite satisfied, Harriet Powers left one final legacy. Having taught herself to read through sheer determination via her enslaver's children—a rare thing for any Black woman at the time, let alone one who was enslaved—Powers wrote and left behind a letter. She references several of her other creations, letting us know that she made at least five quilts, even as early as 1882. Not only did she craft a tapestry of the most exquisite order, capturing the legacy of her life, but she left a record, a secret code to be passed down to all who came after her. In this code she showed the world precisely what "an aged Negro woman"[3] baring her soul—an alchemist weaving gold out of her own fingertips—was capable of.*

Knowing this about Harriet Powers makes me feel capable. It infuses in me not only the tentative seeds of inspiration but also the grounding weight of a responsibility to weave the threads of my story into gold; a tapestry of my own for those who will come after. I wrote this book to bring together stories of Black women's resistance across generations and to highlight their joy. I wrote it in celebration of the past and present stories of (extra)ordinary women turning their pain into acts of glittering defiance; their *reclaiming*, their

---

* Quilting has traditionally been rooted in feminism, used to advance the cause by documenting women's creativity and storytelling skills.

re-creating, and their *resilience*. In doing so, I hope we can permanently correct a historical record, change a narrative, and inspire a generation. This book is a reminder to every single one of us that our stories—our voices—matter. We are part of a legacy delicately woven by the bare hands of generations of women that the world thought it could silence.

For centuries, Black women have been overlooked, downtrodden, and dismissed. They have been sexualized, racialized, and ignored. Culture has often portrayed Black women as a monolith and in terms of victimhood. And yet, what we have not seen—still do not see enough of—are the real women behind the stereotypes radically resisting being spoken for. Throughout this book, I draw together stories of women many have never even heard of who have quietly, and by any means they could, resisted the grasp of dominant narratives intent on their erasure. These women might not have been prominent in the contemporary sense of how we understand power and what it is to have a voice, but they have led lives of determined resistance. In reclaiming their individual acts and voices from the cultural narrative that, for centuries, would rather suppress them, *This Thread of Gold* will make these women visible—in some cases for the very first time. The world will see them rise.

This Thread of Gold travels through time, visiting workplaces, film sets, literary salons, churches, and kitchens. We visit places where resistance took place in whispers from mother to daughter about the art of the possible, where it took place so quietly and subtly that you could be forgiven for not even noticing it—and indeed most people didn't—but also where it happened loudly, exuberantly, and on a global scale. You will meet Black women from Europe, Africa, America, and the Caribbean dating as far back as the eighteenth century. You will discover how these women have used art, the media, politics, food, deadly weapons, and any other available means to challenge the dominant narratives about Blackness and womanhood—and to offer alternative and assertive visions for both.

Black women are not victims. Black women are alchemists, spinning gold from lives of hardship. Their alchemy is born of necessity—a need to break down in order to rebuild and survive. Far from a homogenous assembly, Black women forge new intergenerational stories by drawing together and saying *no*. It will always be important to speak about the oppressions faced by Black women, but *This Thread of Gold* is not here to occupy that space. This book is dedicated solely to Black women surviving, thriving, and glowing.

I first dreamed up this book in 2017 while completing my master's degree in women's studies at the University of Oxford. I was determined to trace a lineage of Black women's history from Aunt Jemima to Beyoncé's *Lemonade*, shining a light on how Black women have used food as a means of resistance. In the eyes of certain senior academics, Oxford University and Beyoncé did not necessarily go together, but I stood my ground and didn't look back, graduating with the highest honors and an even fiercer determination to un-cover more stories, to trace the heritage of the women who formed me.

I have learned about the women you will meet in *This Thread of Gold* through meticulous and determined research, from my own experiences, and from the storytelling of my mother, my grandmother, and the generations of women who came before them. In writing this book, not only am I paying tribute to the grandmothers who have paved the way for its existence, but I am acknowledging that it exists only because they were here first. We are walking their path. They have woven the tapestry, painted the picture that takes us to where we are today. It is our responsibility to pick up this thread.

At its heart, *This Thread of Gold* is a book about connec-tions: what anchors us to our past and what we carry with us into our future. I hope it will also act as a manifesto: a mani-festo for resistance and a manifesto for survival, showing the world how Black women have fundamentally transformed the platitude about what one should do when life hands out lem-ons. Connecting Black women's historical legacy to the future fight that we all need to be a part of, it is time for us to con-tinue the journey, recognize hardship, and elevate each indi-vidual example of survival. After all, why shouldn't Black womanhood be expansive?

Part I

RECLAMATION

*In which we explore how Black women accept
what they cannot change and they reclaim it*

Chapter One

SILENCE

T HIS THREAD OF GOLD that ties me to my mother, my grandmother, and the women who came before looks a lot like the color purple. Like the purple hibiscus as it opens, entering a space that's never been seen before. It is yellow as the fruit of the lemon, it is yellow as the bus that we shall not be moved from, yellow as the lemonade that we make as we take one pint of water and half of a yellow sun and transform the sour into something sustaining. It is red as the umbilical cord that once physically held us, and red like the blood that we bleed. It is green like the gardens of our mothers that we are still in search of and black like the flags that we wave as we frown, buckle down, and plant: bending as we sow, reaching as we climb. It is brown as the soil left down on the ground from the trees that we lift, leaving space for the seedlings to reach to the sun and to grow and to glow as they bask in its shine. Golden. Gold. This thread of gold that ties me to my mother, my grandmother, and the women who came before looks a lot like the color purple.

I am my mother's daughter. I am raised by lionesses. Women as fierce and as mighty as they are brave, as vulnerable and sensitive as they are proud, and as beautiful as they are strong. Sometimes they speak truthfully to those with the power and sometimes they prefer to sit quietly and say nothing at all. Sometimes they say no to expectations and sometimes they say yes and break as they cry, down on the bathroom floor. They are ballet dancers, cat lovers, and video gamers. They are introverts, pioneers, and hopeless romantics. They tell it like it is, but sometimes they don't want to hear it.

I am indelibly linked to a tapestry, rich in its colors and delicate, complex detail. Running through each square is a thread of gold, spun from the silk of the sea—the salt of tears and the sweat that accompanies each loving, labored breath. This thread of gold seems delicate but it cannot and shall not ever be broken, for it holds the tapestry together and it belongs solely to womankind. It is our light. Without this thread of gold, the tapestry is just colors and squares, isolated patchwork cocoons. Without this thread of gold, the tapestry does not exist. It is nothing at all.

My grandmother showed me how to laugh—and keep laughing, no matter what comes my way. My mother taught me humility. My aunties gave me my self-worth, showed me that I was a rare and precious jewel and people should walk across hot coals for me. My cousins taught me how to defend myself, first with my words and then with my fists when necessary: right, left, right (rarely necessary). My sisters taught me when to say sorry, that I do not need to be right all the time. My friends taught me to take care of myself: to rest and to eat and to be gentle, that it mattered less what I did than who I was. These are the threads that are a part of me, woven into the tapestry that is mine, both of me and in me. I hang on to these threads. I cherish them as I understand that one day I will become matriarch of my own pride. I am because of them. They are and they will be because of me. And so, while any good story starts at the beginning, this isn't the beginning because I come from so many women. From the sky to the seabed and every little grain of sand on the shore, this is our story. It is alchemy. It is magic. It is the orchestra soaring in perfect harmony and it is joined together, piece to piece, by this glittering thread of gold.

I've noticed, as I've moved out of my teens and into the complexities of adulthood, that I have started to choose silence. Silence was never something that I chose before. I spoke frequently and loudly, even when I didn't have much to say. In fact, I have lost count of the times that a housemate or a family member remarked on what it is like living with an elephant (annoying, apparently) as I sprint around or thump my way about whichever house I happen to be living in. My mum likes to laugh at me when I go home now, rolling her eyes and telling me, "We do know you're here, Catherine!"

And, as usual, after some time reflecting on it, I think she's right. It is as though I like to remind others and reassure myself that I. Am. Here. I can't be forgotten because look what a vibrant and dazzling human being I am. I want to be seen and I want to be heard. I demand it.

This is why I am perplexed by the fact that in recent years I seem to have stopped talking. I'm not trying to say that I'm suddenly shy. I don't think I ever could be; it's a part of who I am to thrive off human connections. And yet, there has been something subtle and gradual that has happened, leaving me feeling slightly more measured and perhaps a little more timid. I am more careful about what other people are thinking, wondering if they approve, and this has been transformed, somewhere along the way, into my stopping talking. Looking at myself objectively, as though I were a specimen in a test tube, I think there are a number of reasons for this. There was the manager at work who, as I shared my excitement with him about an idea that I'd had, cut me off midsentence and told me that I shouldn't speak so quickly or it would put people off because they would realize how young I was. Then there was the boyfriend who would draw me in close just to see how far away he could throw me, telling me disdainfully that I appeared to have ADHD as I was talking so much and couldn't I just "chill"? Then I had the long months on my own working and traveling, followed by the drama school experience that branded me a troublemaker for asking questions of an outdated institution in a space that didn't encourage them. You name it, I can see where it came from. Whether this was deserved or not and whether I should have listened to the requests that I button my lip and bite my tongue are different questions. What I am clear on, though, is that my newfound silence was directly and causally linked to the more space that I felt I was taking up. In a world that didn't really set out to listen, I was always flirting with the danger of being too loud. And so I learned to arm myself, to opt out and choose silence in certain spaces. The fact that the spaces where I found myself being silenced were both white and almost all male was, until recently, beside the point. Thinking about this now is uncomfortable. I had entered the world and been raised by the lionesses in my family to be exuberant—Catherine Joy White. I lived up to my name. Somewhere along the way I had lost that exuberance. In a world of black and white, I had adopted a decidedly measured shade of gray.

I often think about what happens in the in-between. In the space between infancy, childhood, and adulthood. How do we become? What forms us? If we are created by outside influences that are not our own, then how do they take hold? Where do they come from? Of course, to a certain extent this can be answered by the nature-versus-nurture debate. We are influenced by where we are raised, who we are raised by, and how they raise us. And yet it is far more complex than that. We are also influenced by what people expect of us: where they expect us to live, who they expect us to be, and how they expect us to be that. If we really tried to tune in and listen to all the voices seeking to lay a claim over who we are, it would be deafening. If we tried to answer back and defend ourselves against every misjudged assertion or claim, our voices would be hoarse. Inevitably silence is easier. And yet silence in this context—when it doesn't feel as though it has come around organically—can often taste an awful lot like defeat. It takes a great deal of bravery, and outright defiance, to hear the noise and yet choose silence or to embrace the noise and keep talking regardless.

This has been an ongoing dilemma for me in recent years. It is as though once I entered my mid-twenties the innate confidence of my youth seemed fragile. As I hesitantly navigated this dichotomy, unsure whether my own voice was liberating or choking me, I became more clouded, more unsure about who I was supposed to be. You can imagine my relief then when on September 19, 2021, Michaela Ewuraba Boakye-Collinson, more commonly known as Michaela Coel, spoke about silence in a way that felt as though it had been written just for me.

Coel, writer, lead actor, show runner, executive producer, and director of the groundbreaking series *I May Destroy You*, had just made history at the 73rd Primetime Emmy Awards as the first Black woman ever to win the Emmy Award for Outstanding Writing for a Limited or Anthology Series or Movie. Even before this accolade, Coel was ingrained on my consciousness. Her reflections on her time at drama school had sustained me through my own sometimes miserable training. Coel had experienced for the first time in her life being told that she was too angry and aggressive, observations that belittled her, brought her to tears even, for in her previous experiences working with Black theater companies she had always been praised for her positive energy. When I discovered that the school would cast her in parts to "help" her explore her soft side, I was immediately able to at least resign myself to (if not accept) my own similar drama school experiences. I was given the part of the servant or the narrator with songs to sing about heartbroken, rejected, and lovesick (or even just plain old *sick*) women for the very same reason: I was too fiery. I needed to explore my soft side. I would cast my mind back to just one year earlier when, among my many joyful student drama experiences, I played Rita in *Made in Dagenham*, the role of my dreams.

It was—is—the theater I am drawn to. Bringing to life women who are complex and complicated, and who get things done not by being superheroes, but by embracing the quirks of their own personalities, both their insecurity and their bravery, and doing them anyway. And yet, I arrived at drama school and was forced to sit back and watch other women harness their strength and navigate the limits of human emotion while I donned a servant's uniform and explored my "softness." I got the point. Sometime after that, I just stopped expecting anything different, letting the silence consume me again.

Fast-forward to the end of the year and preparations for our final showcase, the chance to let agents, directors, and producers see our work for the first time. It was a big deal. My friend Bella and I rehearsed a scene together from the film *Belle*, a period drama based on the life of Dido Elizabeth Belle, a British heiress raised in eighteenth-century aristocratic Britain alongside her white cousin Elizabeth. I was drawn to their relationship as an example of friendship—of sisterhood—across a racial divide. It was a hard-hitting scene, exploring how we can choose to wound with our words: jabbing here, stabbing there. But when we showed it to the teachers at drama school for approval before showcase rehearsals began, they asked us to cut the end reference to race. I didn't understand. "But that is the point of the scene. Otherwise it just becomes two young women fighting over a man. It is so much more than that," I argued. Bella was off sick that afternoon, so I stood alone, trying to advocate for what I knew was the story I wanted—needed—to tell. I wouldn't say what I saw in my teacher's eyes was anger. It was colder than that. She told me that my attitude was unacceptable, that I needed to learn some respect, and that she would not tolerate my "behavior." This all unfolded in front of a senior teacher and my entire year group. Every single person stayed silent as I tried to defend my reasoning for why the scene was important— and eventually just tried to defend myself. I left rehearsals that evening in tears.

The next morning that sadness had dissipated. I felt only

fire. After a year of having my voice swallowed up, I realized that I would not find the words in a text already written that could convey what I wanted to say, that really encompassed how loud I wanted to scream. I gave up and wrote my own monologue. It was a little piece called *What If?*, about an eighteen-year-old finally daring to use her voice and talk back to her friend who minimized her achievements by telling her that she got into Cambridge University only because she was Black. It's fairly clumsily written and by no means a work of art, but I am proud of it because for the first time since opting for silence, I spoke back. Inspired by learning that Michaela Coel had also written her own work to perform at her showcase, creating a two-hander for her and Paapa Essiedu (who also stars in *I May Destroy You*) with characters who spoke like them, *I started to write my own story*. When it came to writing *What If?* there was no part of me that associated it with me being revolutionary. At the time, I just knew that nothing I was being given was speaking the words that I wanted to speak in the way that I wanted to speak them. Now, however, I give myself a little more credit, noting that this was an early example of me not seeing myself in the spaces that I occupied and so deciding to write myself in.

Because of all this, by the time Coel made her way onto the stage to accept her Emmy Award, in my mind our experiences were already intertwined. Her words were a part of me, imprinted onto my DNA. As she arrived onstage, she took a moment and then she began to talk. She didn't speak for long and every single word landed like a promise. I watched, holding my breath, as she observed the room filled with glittering stars and heavyweights of the film industry, finally deigning to welcome her in. She saw them and she acknowledged them. But her message was not for them. Michaela Coel looked beyond, raising her gaze and speaking directly to every single person who knew what it is to question the validity of their own voice.

"Write the tale that scares you, that makes you feel uncertain, that isn't comfortable," she challenged. Dedicating her award to every survivor of sexual assault, Coel used the moment to encourage us to move away from the need to be constantly visible. Speaking not to the industry representatives and the Hollywood status quo but instead to those, like me, who were at home choking on their silence and the seeming uselessness of their voice in a world that is deafening, Coel dared us to be brave enough to disappear from the noise at times and "see what comes to you in the silence."

In a way that rarely happens with the typical blah-blah endless thank-you speeches that are the norm at these sorts of events, Michaela Coel took the world by storm. Everywhere I turned people were talking about *that* speech. Of course, winning this award was about Coel: It was long overdue and hugely deserved. But what she really did with her acceptance speech was look away from the noise surrounding— suffocating—each of us and dare us to drown it out. She gave us permission to turn down the volume. What she really did with her Emmy acceptance speech was turn to her audience, extend her hand, and say to us: *This is for you.*

Suddenly, the silence that had been stifling me did not seem so overwhelming. It felt like a considered choice, if I were brave enough to let it become one. So I went away, I shut down all the voices, and I simply dared to let the quiet in. In fact, I did what my mum would cry out for when my sisters and I argued about something ridiculous: I "let the peace of God reign!"

What I found in its space was a compulsion to rewrite my own story. What would my voice sound like if I dared to let it exist undisrupted? The more I thought about this and the more I sat in the space and the silence, examining what re-writing my story might look like, the more I felt a pull to discover if this had ever happened before. Surely Michaela Coel was not the first woman in the world to call for a time-out, to dare to propose an alternative. What about the women who came before her? Did they have someone to challenge them to remove themselves from the noise of the world, or were they just swept away in its cacophony? I started to search for answers, slowly at first, then growing animated the more I discovered as I found that I could trace women from hundreds of years before Coel who wrote, rewrote, and rein-vented the story of their lives, taking a narrative, accepting it, and then reclaiming it for their own as they wove their truths into the tapestry like silk.

I landed on one period in particular: the rapidly changing

end of the nineteenth century, as the new horizons of the twentieth century beckoned. I became fascinated with the stories I uncovered. In the United States, the Civil War had resulted in the end of slavery and Black women found themselves at the heart of discussions being had by white people about what precisely their recently freed "property" should do. Food and culinary practices, in many ways linked to Black women who had worked as nannies and cooks, guided the momentum and direction of these discussions. Freed Black women were relishing their newfound independence and using it to showcase and expand their culinary skills. Having been more than happy to allow Black women to use these skills for their own benefit for the past century, white people responded to this with much concern.

There was almost a sense that the world needed to explain away this anomaly of freed Black women possessing talent and, more important, their ability to showcase these talents, even out of the limited opportunities available to them. Up until this point, culinary talents displayed by Black women had been explained by one time-honored route in particular: the Mammy figure. With stringent criteria—overweight, illiterate, docile, and asexual—a caretaker who cared for the family she was owned by more than she cared for herself, the Mammy had lived and breathed for the previous century primarily as a way of justifying the abominations of slavery. At the end of the Civil War, when slavery was abolished, the Mammy was also set free. Desperate to keep her where she belonged (silenced), the dominant voices shouted even louder and transformed her from Mammy to Aunt Jemima—a commercialized version of her predecessor who sat on top of pancake boxes across America until June 2021. Mammy didn't disappear, she was just given a new name and became even more visible than before.

Born out of the image of the happy, loving Black woman, inseparable from food, Aunt Jemima (personified by nanny, cook, activist, model, and former enslaved woman Nancy Green) burst into the public eye in 1890 and grew to be hugely popular. Her image soon became nationally recognized, appearing on many household goods and reinforcing the idea that meek and silent Black women would selflessly work for white families, happy with any reward that they were given. Across the country, Black women were silenced, hidden behind Aunt Jemima's smiling mask of contentment. Regardless of whether she was called Mammy or Aunt Jemima, the end result remained the same: Even while walking free, Black women continued to be viewed as natural and willing slaves. Even worse, unlike the Mammy, Aunt Jemima did not vanish as public opinion changed. Instead, she remained on those pancake boxes for the next one hundred years. It wasn't until June 17, 2020, following the murder of George Floyd, that news was released regarding the Quaker Oats food company's plans to finally change the Aunt Jemima pancake and syrup name and logo, stating that "we recognize Aunt Jemima's origins are based on a racial stereotype. . . . As we work to make progress toward racial equality . . . we also must take a hard look at our portfolio of brands and ensure they reflect our values."[1]

For over a hundred years, Black women were forced to face slavery's monstrous legacy as they ate their breakfast every morning. It is no wonder then that Aunt Jemima's descendants have continued to declare that they find this unpalatable. However, just like Michaela Coel, unafraid of the silence, Black women paused for a while, contemplating, cooking. And then, quietly as they liked, they mobilized. They used the enforced silence and servitude of their circumstances to rework the image projected on to them and instead created a speaking platform for the many other stories more faithfully representing the diversity of Black women's existence. And, way before the Quaker Oats food company finally decided to move on from the damaging image of their figurehead, they started talking.

There is a collection called *The Black Back-ups* by poet Kate Rushin. Published in 1993 and dedicated to "all of the Black women who sang back-up / For Elvis Presley, John Denver, James Taylor, Lou Reed. / Etc. Etc. Etc.," the title poem offers an alternative image of Aunt Jemima, bringing the real woman behind the fixed smile on the pancake box vividly to life. The poem dedicates itself to the women in Rushin's family, as well as "all of the Black women riding on buses"; "the women who open those bundles of dirty laundry sent home from those ivy-covered campuses"; "Hattie McDaniel . . .

Ethel Waters . . . Saphronia."[2] (McDaniel is the actor who played Mammy in *Gone with the Wind*, a role she was criticized for within the Black community. Waters is a singer and actress, the first African-American woman to be nominated for an Emmy Award, and Saphronia is a character in Nina Simone's revolutionary song "Four Women," which details the lives of four Black women grappling with their quest for self-identification.)

The poem then moves on to "Aunt Jemima," who is referred to in a teasing taunt as the words and phrases run into each other, moving from the general observation about Aunt Jemima on the pancake box to it being woven into something personal, transforming from "AuntJemimaonthepancakebox?" into "ain't chure Mama on the pancake box?" The poem goes on to then ask one's mama to come off the box and rejoin the family at home.

Reading it for the first time really stopped me in my tracks, reminding me that behind the symbol of Aunt Jemima lies a real person, often someone's mother or wife or sister. It refuses to allow us to let any of these women remain a faceless, voiceless shape. Rushin takes this even further and creates a world where far from just grinning inanely from the pancake box, Aunt Jemima works as a nurse, saving lives. She goes to prayer meetings on Wednesdays and rushes around; she is a whirlwind of personality and color fighting back against the fabricated concoction that has been placed on her.

There's another poem, written in 1983 by poet Sylvia

Dunnavant, called "Aunt Jemima on the Pancake Box." It opens with the question "Does anybody know what ever happened to Aunt Jemima on the pancake box?" The response makes me get up out of my seat and cheer as the narrator weaves a world where Aunt Jemima "got tired of wearing that rag wrapped around her head. / And she got tired of making pancakes and waffles for other people to eat while she couldn't sit down at the table." And, in a blazing display of fiery autonomy, a woman writing her own story, she told our narrator that: "Lincoln emancipated the slaves / but she freed her own damn self." In a final flourish we learn that "the last time I saw Aunt Jemima / She was driving a Mercedes-Benz / with a bumper sticker on the back that said / 'free at last, free at last, / thank God all mighty / I am free at last.'"

What a ferocious reclamation. Not only do these poems show Aunt Jemima as nothing more than a construct, silencing Black women without their permission, they also highlight her for what she was: a continuation of slavery. I like to think that long before Quaker Oats finally made moves to remove Aunt Jemima from the pancake box, Black women such as Sylvia Dunnavant and Kate Rushin had already been freeing their own damn selves. The most powerful thing about all of this is that as these women shed their shackles, not only do they rewrite their own identities, they pave the way for future generations of Black women to define themselves, allowing nothing and no one to force them into a box that they do not want to inhabit. Instead, Black women such as Rushin and Dunnavant have put themselves at the heart of the story that had been wrongly written about them, and in a rush of righteous fury, they have stepped off the pancake box, neither enslaved nor bound to any one mode of being, but vibrant and liberated women.

The more I dive into this reclaiming of the real woman behind the image on the pancake box, the more I realize the importance of uncovering—and of naming. Nancy Green, the real Aunt Jemima, who sat on top of those pancake boxes for the best part of a century, no longer exists in the kitchens of every American. But the complexity of losing her image also means that, paradoxically, she has been lost too, fading into obscurity rather than being given the very public recognition that befits someone of her stature. The real Nancy Green was a Black storyteller and one of the first Black corporate models to exist in the United States. She used her profile to advocate against poverty and in support of creating equal rights for all in Chicago. She was also a philanthropist and a church leader, one of the founding members of the oldest active Black Baptist church in Chicago. After her death, she was buried in an unmarked grave, where she remained until 2015. Then, after a fifteen-year search, her resting place was rediscovered by a woman called Sherry Williams, founder of the Bronzeville / Black Chicagoan Historical Society. Williams had worked backward, using the only bit of knowledge that she had for certain—the date of Green's death—to communicate with the Oak Woods Cemetery staff and locate the plot of land where Green had been lying with no marker since her death in 1923. Fascinated by Green's life and disturbed by this American icon lying forgotten with no recognition, Williams determined to honor her with a headstone. Romi Crawford, professor at the School of the Art Institute of Chicago, supported the cause, hoping that Green would go on to be remembered for more than just playing a racist stereotype. She stated that: "The problem with the portrayal is that she was, and Black women subsequently are, plagued by representations that don't align with the scope of their ambition, desires and abilities. . . . Knowing her story will help debunk the caricature."[3]

I reflect on this, grappling for the first time with how important it is to speak out into the silence, paint the full picture—or risk forever remaining a mask of enforced contentment, a false image on a pancake box. As part of her mission, Williams reached out to Quaker Oats to ask whether they would support a movement in favor of placing a headstone on Green's grave. They responded simply that "Nancy Green and Aunt Jemima aren't the same. . . . Aunt Jemima is a fictitious character." In other words, they washed their hands of any responsibility. In return, Williams stated her desire that rather than simply removing the logo and pretending that it never existed, Quaker Oats would work to ensure that women such as Green—whom they had profited from enormously—would not be forgotten. "Instead of spending the money on new packaging, put some narrative about the role of Black women in taking care and feeding this nation from enslavement to now. . . . And educate [consumers] about Nancy Green herself, whose likeness was used for this package,"[4] she wrote. Nancy Green's life is part of the legacy of America. Her thread runs through the tapestry, binding it with kindness and a fierce sense of justice. Where she was not able to reclaim her own story, Sherry Williams stepped in. It is our collective responsibility to take up that thread.

Reading between the lines of these reclamations, from Kate Rushin to Sylvia Dunnavant to piecing together the real Nancy Green via Sherry Williams's careful investigation, I began to see myself in a new way. I slowly started to understand that without even comprehending my actions or motivations, I had already been reclaiming my narrative, snatching it back from the clutches of those who sought to take it from my possession. In every situation I'd been in that had silenced me, I had found a way of speaking into the void. I didn't forget about that manager at work who told me I talked too quickly. How could I? In fact, after years of second-guessing my authority, perpetually afraid of appearing too young to be taken seriously, I found myself being interviewed live on American TV for International Women's Day 2021, talking about the impact of COVID-19 on women. Just before they called "action," I paused, reminding myself to talk slowly and imbue myself with gravitas and weight. But then, as I thought about my manager and what he would think of me, I looked at the camera and started to think about who I was really speaking for. I felt a lightness—a weightlessness—begin to grow, and with what I now recognize to be my style when speaking in public, I infused my words with my passion, speaking quickly but bringing my audience in with me, trusting in my own voice. When the inevitable happened and things went south with that boyfriend (Mr. "Why-Can't-You-Just-*Chill?*") I was shattered. But then, rebuilding slowly from something that had very nearly left me physically and mentally broken, I began to find my voice again. I coined my (now legendary among my friends) hashtag: #shinebrightlikecatwhite. Ask anyone I went to university with what song reminds them of me and they will tell you without even thinking: "Titanium" by David Guetta featuring Sia. With lyrics such as "I'm bulletproof, nothing to lose, fire away, fire away"[5] . . . you get the picture. I had been rewriting my story without even realizing it. I didn't have to be the little girl I had once been, nor did I have to be the adult I had been molded into. I was giving myself (or taking) permission to allow for time and space to write and rewrite my own story. And actually, it didn't have to be a masterpiece. It just had to be my voice.

Some years ago, when Michaela Coel was the first Black woman in the then forty-two-year history of the MacTaggart lecture series to deliver a speech, she used it to reflect on how important it is that "voices used to interruption get the experience of writing something without interference at least once."[6] I feel that in my gut. I am allowed to write—and to speak—without being interrupted. This is my part of the tapestry and I am weaving it out of finest gold.

I count myself lucky to belong to a generation of people who can look up to someone like Michaela Coel. I followed her example and she made me brave. One of the things I love most about I May Destroy You (and there are many) is how Coel genuinely doesn't shy away from the fact that life is complex. Nothing is black and white—how can it be? This sounds like an obvious thing to say, but that has not stopped us from neatly categorizing things and ideas and situations in a way that helps us understand them. What this has meant for groups in society who are not the mainstream voice is that being heard often goes hand in hand with a distasteful compulsion to make sure that we remain palatable to write a masterpiece. We've got a seat at the table—just—but it takes every inch of our concentration and physical strength to hang on to it. We had better not slip up by wearing the wrong thing or forgetting what we're holding on to, because if we do, we will fall—and it will hurt. Michaela Coel faces this head-on and fearlessly makes work that also highlights her own complexities as much as it elevates her voice. Arabella, the protagonist of I May Destroy You, is fiercely complex. She is charismatic, defiant—and broken. We are rooting for Arabella, obviously, but if anything we champion her more because she is not perfect. Coel does not need us to like Arabella. Michaela Coel doesn't even need us to like Michaela Coel.

This isn't an easy thing to achieve because we are innately human and both our DNA and the way modern society is built function around finding others who want to be near us, who approve of us. But when you really think about it, being liked isn't exactly the point. Actually, we can find our greatest freedom from shutting down the noise, stepping out of this need to be palatable and being brave enough to put our own fears aside, in the hope that by doing so we might also uplift someone else. That is how we really reclaim—and eventually rewrite—the narrative. What if we dared to do that? *What if?*

Chapter Two

DEFIANCE

J UST BEFORE I TURNED twenty-one, I was asked a question
that I did not, for the life of me, have any idea how to answer. I was in the Caribbean, far from home, and to be perfectly honest, I was struggling. I was finishing my year abroad
in the French-speaking Caribbean islands—"les départements
d'outre-mer"—and was staying with a Guadeloupean woman
called Jacqueline. We had been working together in Paris and
became very close that year. She had been living away from
her husband and her family home in Guadeloupe so that her
son could attend school in France. I'd been living in a foreign
country for the first time, finding my feet independently of
my family and all that had previously been a defining part of
my identity. Jacqueline was kindly and protective toward me,
seeing me in many ways as a replacement daughter. She even
jokingly called me her "fille adoptive." So when I told her that

I wanted to spend some time in Guadeloupe, she welcomed me into her home with open arms. Despite her kindness, life was tough for me out there. Her house was remote. Without a car it was impossible for me to get around. I set myself milestones: save up enough money to rent a car and then rent my own small room somewhere in one of the larger cities. I worked toward these goals and got through each day, but inside I was lonely and deeply miserable. Outwardly my body reflected this too as I became dangerously thin. My only solace was my daily routine of a run and a swim, and I would often lie in that beautiful water, floating on the idyllic Caribbean Sea, and curse myself for the bitter, heavy feeling in my stomach as I watched each airplane fly over my head and wished I could be on it. I knew I should be happy; I was quite literally in paradise, living what for many people could only be described as a dream, and therefore I could not entertain an existence where I allowed anything less than euphoria to come through. Although I tried to hide these feelings, desperate as ever to give the impression that I was thriving, Jacqueline would notice and encourage me to talk. We were close like a mother and daughter at that point—and I very much fulfilled the role of moody teen. I was a confusing mixture of sharp retorts with excessive politeness, and most notably, I never quite managed to let down my guard enough to really engage with her. I couldn't bear for her—or anyone—to think that I was anything less than fine. Eventually, frustrated, she straight-out asked me: "What is it you feel you have to prove?" I couldn't answer. I think about that question a lot, often as I catch myself yet again doing more, needing to prove myself in some strange way for some pointless reason time and time again. *Why?* I ask myself. *Why can't I let people see me just as I am? What am I so afraid of? What do I have to prove?*

I am not alone in this feeling. Many women feel that they need to work twice as hard to be taken half as seriously. For Black women, these feelings are often even more extreme. There is a sense that we have to be strong, that we have to be the most talented in the room, blazing a trail with our brilliance, and eventually this feeling starts to grind us down. It starts to encourage others to have wholly unrealistic expectations of us. It starts to make us feel disappointed with ourselves when we don't meet these expectations, even if we're already giving more than we can muster. At twenty-one, I had barely begun to recognize the harm that this sentiment was doing to me. I was in the Caribbean alone, learning French, earning my own money by doing research for a small company, and living my best life. I. Was. Fine. Except, I wasn't—or I didn't have to be all the time. It is okay not to enjoy every single experience. Sometimes things just don't work out. It's also okay to walk away from them. But I didn't know that, or I couldn't see it at the time.

Just as Jacqueline refuted the notion that I always had to be on top, daring me to defy it, so do we need to defy it—for ourselves and for each other. It is time to reject the harmful notion that Black women have to be strong (whatever "strong" may mean). Resistance and resilience do not always have to mean strength. The idea of the perpetually strong Black woman is a myth, and a harmful one. The "strong Black woman" is a trope that has been created, a one-dimensional narrative that still dominates. Two hundred years ago this myth was the "Mammy" raising white children by day before going home at night to tend to her own. Today, this myth has been translated into the single mothers raising entire households, the carers and nurses who smilingly and uncomplainingly give to others with never a thought for themselves. The Black women politicians who all too often are the "first" at something and face monumental abuse because of it. The Black women who are the bedrock of the family unit. The women who are talked over, talked at, and ignored. They do not hurt. They feel no pain. Their "strength" is their greatest, most glorious asset. This needs to end right here. These women are not real. Worse, in upholding such images, we pass on the impossible standard to ourselves that we too have something to prove: a notion that is intrinsically incorrect. Black women are strong—we have had to be—but we are strong in nuanced ways. Our strength can mean whatever we choose it to. We are alchemists, and we reject any attempt to define us.

Congresswoman Shirley Anita Chisholm carries what I see as the dual honor and burden of being the first Black woman to be elected into the US House of Representatives. Born in 1924 in Brooklyn, New York, Chisholm spent the early years of her life in Barbados, where she was raised by her maternal grandmother. She credits this upbringing and the influence of her grandmother with teaching her to know— and trust—her own voice, refusing to be defined by either her Blackness or her womanhood. In an interview with *The New York Times* she shared proudly: "Granny gave me strength, dignity and love. I learned from an early age that I was some-body. I didn't need the Black revolution to tell me that."[1] So the thread of gold—an uncompromising sense of self and a drive to change the world—was already woven into Chisholm by her grandmother.

At school she was academically gifted and from as early as her college years was a member of the Harriet Tubman Soci-ety, working to advocate for causes that would further racial advancement and wider societal inclusion, such as Black sol-diers being able to fight in the military during World War II and more women being able to serve in student government. She married in the late 1940s and worked during her early years as a nursery school teacher, going on to become an au-thority on child welfare issues.

Chisholm moved into the world of politics in the 1950s, when she worked to support an organization's effort to elect the first Black judge in Brooklyn, before eventually leaving the group when they limited the decision-making abilities of their female members. Wanting more than to simply be a passive member, she moved to a new organization, the Unity Demo-cratic Club, and campaigned for Thomas Jones to become

Brooklyn's second Black assemblyman. In 1964, when Jones accepted a judicial position rather than running for reelection, Chisholm stepped up to another level: She decided to run for his seat. Faced with resistance at almost every angle as a woman—and a Black woman at that—Chisholm persevered and won the Democratic primary in June of that year. Then, in November, the remarkable happened. She won the seat with a majority of over eighteen thousand votes.

She immediately set to work, implementing groundbreaking, radical change as she went. In 1968, with the deliciously fist-pumping campaign slogan "Unbought and Unbossed"—also the title of her autobiography—Chisholm announced that she would be running for the US House of Representatives and went on to win by approximately a two-to-one margin, making her the first Black congresswoman in the history of the United States of America. As she got started with her new mission, Chisholm worked to lift others up with her, hiring only women for her office, half of whom were Black. When challenged on her plans, she retorted: "I have no intention of just sitting quietly and observing. I intend to . . . focus attention on the nation's problems."[2] This is precisely what she did, implementing over fifty pieces of legislation championing the underdogs: everything and everyone from gender and race equality to enhancing educational attainment among disadvantaged groups to improving the lives of the poor and even working to end the Vietnam War. She pushed for increases in funding to enable more federally funded day-care hours as well as a minimum annual income for families.

Buoyed by the groundbreaking progress she was making, Chisholm launched her highest bid yet: a run for president in the 1972 election. Her quest was marred from the start by criticism and discrimination. She was blocked from participating in any televised primary debates—her response was to sue the Democratic Party, a move that only slightly enhanced her position: She was permitted to make just one speech. Despite this, she still garnered significant support from women, students, and other minority groups, recognizing that they were being overlooked by the other candidates. Largely thanks to this mobilization, she managed to enter twelve primaries and gain 10 percent of the total vote, despite a campaign with significantly less financing than that of her opponents and with contention at each stage from the men around her.

In spite of her ultimately unsuccessful run for the presidency, Chisholm had made history. She was not deterred by what some may view as a defeat and continued to serve in Congress and to surprise everyone around her—from visiting her segregationist rival George Wallace in the hospital after he was shot by a would-be assassin, to fighting for reproductive rights as an essential part of healthcare when this was not a priority (or even a respected) issue. She had a heightened awareness of how the second-wave feminism of the time gave more space to the plight of middle-class women than their working-class counterparts. The movement prioritized causes such as the adoption of the term "Ms." and Chisholm, ever aware that this did not speak specifically to the reality of the experiences—and needs—of the majority of women, made it her mission to broaden the scope of the conversation. In her later years, Chisholm retired from Congress, going on to teach as well as to co-found the National Political Congress of Black Women. When speaking of her legacy, Chisholm stated that she wanted to be "remembered as a woman . . . who dared to be a catalyst of change."[3] One of my favorite quotes of hers is, "If they don't give you a seat at the table, bring a folding chair."[4] Those are words I return to when I need to imbue myself with courage for some daunting task that lies ahead of me.

Chisholm's thread is ebullient, shining. The legacy she dreamed of lives on in Black women throughout history who have followed her lead, taking up her golden trail, parking their chairs and refusing to move them. British politician Diane Abbott is one such individual. She is the first Black woman elected to the UK Parliament and the longest-serving Black MP in the House of Commons, having served Hackney North and Stoke Newington since 1987. Her achievements don't stop there: She can hold her head high and say that she is one of the MPs who voted against the Iraq War and who frequently votes in favor of higher benefits for those who can't work due to sickness or disability. She is fervently and fiercely pro-choice. She founded the London Schools and the Black Child initiative to raise educational achievements among Black pupils in London. Abbott studied at Cambridge University, an education that instilled in her the belief that she belongs in any room she wants to enter and deserves a seat at any table. After giving birth on a Monday (the whips insisting that she work until the Thursday before), she returned to Parliament eight days later. Her son holds the record of being the youngest person to enter a division lobby in the House of Commons. She is a complex and talented woman whose biggest dream was inspired by Nobel Prize–winning author Toni Morrison, who once said, "If you find a book you really want to read, but it hasn't been written yet, then you must write it." The book that Diane Abbott wanted to read, just like Shirley Chisholm before her, told a story never seen before, where a Black woman could be a member of the UK Parliament. And that is precisely what Diane Abbott did.

Since then, she has been besieged by brutal criticism, some of it merited but most of it not. She has been called everything from an "extremist" by her opponents to a "liability" by the Labour Party, her own political party. She spoke out a little about some of the abuse she had faced, detailing how someone had called her (and look away now if you do not want to see some distressing language): a "pathetic useless fat Black piece of shit Abbott. Just a piece of pig shit pond slime who should be fucking hung (if they could find a tree big enough to take the fat bitch's weight)."[5] She has been consistently and relentlessly abused. And yet she has defied all of these labels, continuing to ride the wave, to keep fighting, and to do what she set out to do, which is to fulfill the requirements of the job that she loves, even when it seems like an utterly thankless task.

In the run-up to the 2017 UK general election, Abbott had a string of interviews that can be described as nothing less than a car crash. Even watching them again now, safe in the knowledge that their excruciatingly torturous pain is over, feels genuinely upsetting. In one, she is asked how her government plans to fund ten thousand new police officers and she struggles to explain it, giving wrong figures, pausing, shuffling papers, and laughing nervously. Obviously, the media had a field day. And yet, Abbott later recounted that this had been her seventh interview that morning. She hadn't given incorrect figures in any of her other interviews. She was quite literally exhausted. In a later interview, Abbott was unable to answer questions about a significant report on how to protect London from terror attacks. She assured the interviewer that she had read the report but was unable to remember its recommendations. Jeremy Corbyn, leader of the Labour Party at that time, later announced that Abbott was unwell and was temporarily stepping aside as shadow home secretary. Journalist Gaby Hinsliff wrote at the time in an astute observation: "It's likely that some . . . of those enthusiastically sharing 'gotcha!' interviews on Facebook are more interested in seeing a Black woman publicly humiliated than in the niceties of the

Harris report on counter-terrorism."[6] This was particularly well observed. Other (white male) political figures had made significant blunders. Her political opponent, Tory chancellor Philip Hammond, underestimated the cost of a high-speed railway by more than twenty billion pounds, but that barely made the news. Far from simply holding her to account as all MPs rightfully should be, the criticism surrounding Abbott had moved toward something far more sinister and unpleasant that was obvious to most watching it. It was a witch hunt.

However, despite all of this, in May 2017 the seemingly unthinkable happened. Abbott was reelected to her seat of Hackney North and Stoke Newington, receiving 75 percent of the constituency's votes with an increased majority of over thirty-five thousand. I remember waking up that morning, seeing the news, and feeling goose bumps prickle my entire body. I just kept reading that headline over and over again, filled with an emotion that I couldn't articulate. "The electorate recognize bullying when they see it," my dad said. More to the point, it was such an obvious outpouring of support, an entire constituency pulling up in recognition of a woman who had stayed strong through thirty years of abuse and misogynoir even though she must have felt utterly broken inside. There was a social media post that I loved so much at the time that I had it as the background on my phone for the months following the election. "When you come at the Queen you best not miss,"[7] it read, over an image of Abbott's groundbreaking landslide broken down into deliciously satisfying numbers. It was one of those moments when I felt genuinely proud to be British. They had come for the queen and they had missed by quite the margin. Abbott had stepped back to recover, and like a groundswell beneath her feet, her Hackney constituents had raised her above it all, supporting her when her legs could no longer carry her. Obviously Diane Abbott is a strong woman. That much goes without saying. She would not have withstood such abuse for as long as she has if she wasn't strong. At the same time, strength doesn't mean an inability to feel pain. It doesn't mean that Diane Abbott didn't go home at night, read things about herself online, and cry. For how could she be anything other than broken by what she faced? She's human. Strength is essential for getting things done—it's just that it isn't the only way, nor is it the only characteristic that we possess. It doesn't define us.

Abbott touched on this in a 2017 interview with *The Voice*, stating that: "People always talk about strong Black women, and I'm sick of hearing that because everyone is human. . . . Contrary to what you've heard about strong Black women, even strong Black women cry, even strong Black women feel alone, even strong Black women wonder, 'Is this all really worth it?'"[8] It's a powerful question. Following Meghan Markle's Oprah interview in 2021, where she admitted that she had considered taking her own life, Abbott seemed to shed further light on her response, speaking out about her own experiences and stating that she hoped it would show Black and biracial women that they do not need to suffer in silence. Abbott, who in the run-up to the 2017 general election received nearly half of all the abusive messages sent to female MPs in the UK, told *The Guardian* in 2021, "One of the most upsetting things is when people, meaning well, will say: 'Oh, but, Diane, you're so strong.' Nobody is that strong. Nobody can take the sort of abuse that Meghan had to take and that I've had to take. And by dismissing it by saying: 'Oh, Black women are strong,' that's denying our humanity."[9] Recognizing this and speaking candidly about it was possibly one of the bravest things Abbott did.

I am, by anyone's definition, busy. I hold down five full-time jobs: a *Forbes* 30 Under 30–honored actor, writer, film-maker, CEO of a film production company, and gender adviser to the United Nations as well as multiple side hustles, freelance work, and non-work-related commitments, the last standing at any party. There is no escaping the fact that I am living life to its most extreme and in recent years I have heard more times than I can count sentences along the lines of "You're literally Superwoman, I don't know how you do it." That sort of thing. The answer, I often want to scream, is not necessarily because I want to. It's because I put off thinking about my mental health as much as I possibly can. It's because I put work above almost everything and I run marathons in order to tire my body out so much that I don't have to listen to my thoughts. It's because I sleep lightly, wake often, and pull my hair out because my own hands don't know how to do nothing at all. I dance with the danger of burnout because

I don't know how *not* to be busy. I don't know who I would find there.

Society places expectations on each of us that make it feel as though we have something to prove. This leaves us feeling like we can't open up about our mental health because people depend on us to be the strong ones when, in fact, sometimes we want someone to ask us: "How are you *really* doing today?" And then, when we tell them, we want them to raise us up, hold us, and cherish us tenderly while we recover. That's how I see what Abbott's Hackney constituents did for her in that election. I smile to myself as I remember that when she was forced to apologize after (shock, horror) being caught drinking a Marks & Spencer mojito on a London Overground train, M&S sold out of them the next day. Writer Philippa Perry said: "Oh mate. We've all done it. Anyway thanks for traveling on the tube like most people have to do." And Labour MP David Lammy posted: "Jah Rastafari! Why was the rum not Jamaican?"[10] We are here to support each other, to raise each other up. But also, it means a lot when others come and join the fight, when it is a collective effort.

I think as far as being a good ally is concerned, recognizing the consequences of the trope of the strong Black woman is a really useful place to start. According to Guilaine Kinouani, a psychologist, founder of Race Reflections, and author of *Living While Black*, these consequences range "from us being less likely to be seen as vulnerable thus not picked up for depression . . . to being allocated the most difficult and risky tasks or clients at work, to being maligned when we attempt to be vulnerable, all the way to us being less likely to receive anesthesia and pain medication."[11]

I recently attended a talk with Akua Gyamfi, founder of the online talent directory the British Blacklist. She was on a panel with Marvyn Harrison, founder of Dope Black Dads, and Ayo Akinwolere, presenter and world-record-holding swimmer. Both men talked openly and honestly about their therapists and the positive impact that speaking with their therapists has had on their lives. Akua, though, the only woman on the panel, had never been to therapy. She shared with us that she doesn't like feeling vulnerable and spoke to a resounding chorus of yeses from the women in the audience that Black women are patient with Black men but Black men could exercise more patience with Black women. I was left hugely affected by her words. We encourage Black men to open up about their feelings in any way that we can (and rightly so, for the constraints placed on Black men and the incessant pressures of an inescapable masculinity that must be adhered to at all costs place undue harm on Black men and boys across the world). However, that same encouragement to open up and to share—to be vulnerable—does not always apply to Black women. Speaking with Akua afterward gave me such an intensely connected feeling. I shared with her how I too had never properly "done therapy"—through a mixture of not having time and I guess also not necessarily being willing or able to dive too deep into my vulnerabilities. I don't think I want to be like this forever, though. I hope that one day this might change.

It is time to shift away from this narrative that prohibits Black women from being able to experience the full range of their feelings. Resilience is woven into our DNA. We wear it proudly, and yet we must not be afraid of sharing our pain. The world must stop ignoring us when we cry. Black women are not victims, but nor are we superheroes. It hurts when we bleed. We must not shy away from this truth, but rather hold it to the light and celebrate Black women against the backdrop of their complexity, their vulnerability, and their humanity. It is unfathomable to me that this is something that still has to be said. After all, if we are just busy being "strong" all the time, then how on earth are we supposed to find the time to be anything else? How are we even supposed to be ourselves?

The other thing is that sometimes when you allow yourself a moment to falter, to weep, to outright scream, you often naturally come back stronger. It can leave you with the restored energy needed to be able to go farther than you would have gone before. Diane Abbott stepped back and her people stepped up, leading to her biggest victory yet. Breaking down can sometimes be the making of you.

Georgia native Stacey Abrams has lived this in full force throughout her career. In 2018, Abrams blazed a trail as the first Black woman to win a primary in a gubernatorial race and become her party's nominee for governor. She was running against Republican Brian Kemp. The campaign was mired in controversy because during his time in office as Georgia's secretary of state, Kemp had canceled more than a million voter registrations. His explanation was that this was due to "inactivity" or error and that he was simply keeping voting records up to date, but Abrams saw this as his stripping over a million Georgia residents of their right to vote. Kemp eventually went on to win the race by just over fifty thousand votes, leading Abrams to believe that his voter suppression had cost her the election. It is a testament to what a force of nature Abrams is that she has managed to transform this bitter defeat into one of her biggest achievements.[12]

In her own words: "I sat shiva for 10 days. Then I started plotting."[13] Abrams went on to lead a crusade against voter suppression and registered eight hundred thousand voters in Georgia; 45 percent of those new voters were under the age of thirty and 49 percent were people of the global majority.[14] And then, in November 2020, Georgia turned blue for the first time since 1992 and Donald Trump was forced out of the White House. With Joe Biden defeating him by fewer than twelve thousand votes, every single vote Abrams registered contributed to that victory. Biden acknowledged Abrams too, declaring: "Let's hear it for Stacey Abrams. Nobody, nobody in America has done more for the right to vote than Stacey. Stacey, you are changing Georgia. You have changed America."[15]

Since then, Abrams has risen to be something of a national figure, becoming one of her party's most prominent members. She even predicts that by the year 2040 she will be elected president of America. On that we will have to watch this space, but what is clear is that Stacey Abrams hit rock bottom but refused to be left on the floor. Georgia resident Kristin Hunt told the BBC: "She could have just sat back and been like, 'Man, I lost.' But she turned it into a W [a win] and she went into it, pushing forward and trying to do better for herself and our community."[16]

Not only did Abrams achieve a victory that is both personal and political, she also achieved something much more difficult: She got into the mindsets of Black voters in the state. She showed them the power of their individual votes and the simple truth that every single one matters. Through her hard work she empowered an entire generation of mostly young and Black voters. In Georgia, Abrams's name is now invoked as a verb meaning to "get things done."

I think about this breaking down and then getting things done a lot, reflecting on how I see it play out in my own life. One time that sticks in my mind was a balmy evening in 2020. I had just gotten in from a run and was about to make some dinner when I got a text from my aunt. My cousin was in trouble with the law, she told me. Would I be free for a family Zoom the next day? "Of course," I replied with a sinking feeling in my heart. When you hear that your family member is in trouble with the law it is never a good thing;

when that family member is a young Black man you are already accepting the inevitable.

The next day, I sat in my garden and saw my family members log on one username at a time—apart and alone in our little squares but together, very much together. I watched my aunts, the matriarchs, as Auntie Nomie relayed the news. The words blurred into one cacophonous sound as she described the chain of events leading up to my cousin's arrest.

I looked at my family, in their little squares across the country—Birmingham, Northampton, Newport, Cardiff—and I saw their faces move from fear to shock to disbelief to sorrow. I watched them crumple, fall in on themselves as their world imploded once again. My uncle had died, without any warning, at the start of 2020, and now, just months after losing their brother, his sisters were faced with losing his son. My heart ached as I saw their pain. My mum, as ever, kept her feelings to herself as she watched her sisters fall apart. But then, one by one, I watched my aunts pull themselves together, get in formation, and face what needed to be done.

"Who is his lawyer?" Auntie Val wanted to know. "Can we find that out?" Nicole, my thirty-something-year-old cousin, the next generation, was already ice cool with the facts. "We already know the system will be against him," she said. "What can we do to make it better?" It is this, I think, that stayed with me, reverberating in my mind for days after that Zoom call on an innocuous Saturday in July. *What can we do to make it better?* Any family who has ever had to hear the news that their loved one is in trouble—and for something potentially serious—will have experienced the range of emotions that hit you like a train. There is something about hearing that news when you're Black that already prepares you for the worst. We could have very easily broken into pieces and stayed shattered. But what good would that have done? I watched my aunts—five sisters situated across the country—mobilize into action. This is not to say that they didn't hurt—for they did, and I watched them, albeit briefly, allow themselves to fall apart. But then, in front of my eyes, these matriarchs pulled together and began making lemonade. Just like Stacey Abrams, they sat shiva . . . and then the plotting began.

Within the space of that hour-long Zoom, we found out how we could contact my cousin as he waited in prison and a plan was made to find out who his legal representation was and how to get him better lawyers if they weren't up to scratch. Most important, though, we were to write to him and call. "Emails are getting him through," Auntie Nomie said between tears. *This is why I love my family*, I thought. They will never leave me alone when I need them. They will always have my back. I rarely open up about how I'm feeling, especially when I am feeling something less than glorious. There was something about seeing the now hackneyed phrase "it's okay not to be okay" brought to life in that moment that has sustained me, made me want to do better. I'm working on allowing myself to fail and to break—and to be okay with that. I'm not there yet, but I do see that I am surrounded by people who would catch me, and that is a powerful feeling.

Miss Major Griffin-Gracy, often just referred to as Miss Major—or these days as "Mama"—is a trans woman activist and community leader for transgender rights who embodies this spirit of never leaving her family behind. Among many other things, she served as the original executive director for the Transgender Gender-Variant & Intersex Justice Project, which aims to help transgender people who are hugely over-represented in the prison systems. This determination to help others like her, to mobilize in support of them, was born from Miss Major herself spending several stints in prison in the seventies. She has been everything from someone who was only able to survive due to state handouts, to a sex worker, to being homeless, to being locked up in prison. As she later discussed openly, it is very difficult not to end up in prison when you are disenfranchised with no access to the "acceptable" means of survival. I would take this one step further and add that it is very difficult to survive when you are disenfranchised. Full stop. Period.

In 1970, at one of Miss Major's lowest points, her close friend was murdered in her apartment and despite a great deal of evidence to the contrary, the police labeled it as a suicide. This made Miss Major realize, quite simply, that those on the margins needed to look out for each other. She described how she started paying careful attention to the well-being of the women she worked the streets with. They all made a pact to write down as much information as possible about any customer one of them got in a car with. They would make the customer step out of the car to discuss the job at hand, as opposed to simply rolling down the window. This meant that any potential murderer or rapist or anyone who meant harm had been seen and logged. If one of the women didn't come home, an entire army of sisters had witnessed the face of the last person to see her alive.[17]

I think of my own experiences, the experiences of so many of my friends—most of us, in fact—taking photos of vehicle registration plates and sending them on before we get in a car, sharing our trips with friends, always making sure to tell each other that we love each other that one time too often, just in case we don't make it back home. These are dark times, born out of misogyny, violence, and trauma, but they also show the power of the collective and of holding each other up when we can no longer hold ourselves. They show us that what we have unquestioningly been doing every time we head back from a night out, or to a friend's house, or even just attempt to walk home, our ancestors have been doing it before us. And they are walking with us now.

Without even realizing it, we cling to them just as we cling to each other, connected by a thread as we hold our hands to our necks and choke every single time one of us does not make it home. We are connected by a thread that holds us together as we work twice as hard to be taken half as seriously. That same thread connects us when we feel, somewhere low in our bellies, the fear of bringing life into the world only to risk our own in the process. We feel it lower still as they shoot dirty words at our matriarchs like bullets. These are our leaders. They walked so that we could run, and now we watch them left bleeding and maimed by faceless cowards hiding behind usernames. When they shoot one of us down they shoot us all. But what they don't realize is that we are connected by a thread as we fight back, every time we organize as they try to silence our voices, stunt our pride, and disconnect us from the power, turning it off at the switch so that nobody will hear our cry. They forgot that within our own two hands we have the power to weave light from the ice of the darkness they left when they shut out the sun. They forgot that even when they take us from the street as we walk to meet a friend, walk home, simply sleep in our own apartments—even as they take us out of this world with no way back in—we are still connected by a thread. They forgot that we will keep raising our voices. We are connected by a thread that anchors us and comforts us as we scream with the sorrow of an army of women burned until our voices are hoarse that *we want to survive*.

They keep trying. But they will never cut this thread. It is woven from sorrow, from the salt of the sea, and we spin it today, propelled and pulled as much by what anchors us to the tapestry as to the delicate nectar of the change that lies ahead. There is a faint light in the distance and we know that it is ours. We know that if we just keep spinning, just keep weaving, then the salt in our hands will eventually, overwhelmingly, irrevocably, transform into the finest shimmering gold. When you come at the queen, you best not miss.

Chapter Three

REINVENTION

Growing up, I was endlessly frustrated by the fact that whenever I would go to my mum expecting sympathy—for playground disputes, teenage fallouts, or boyfriends who wronged me—she would respond without fail by first asking: "And what did you do?" No matter how much I might wish otherwise, my mum is not one of those parents who assumes that her child (or indeed anyone) emerges from a situation in a default position of being right. She wants to know about the nuances, the murky shades of gray. She is interested in the thing you said last week, now long forgotten in your mind but a contributing factor in why your friend is (in your eyes irrationally) hurt that you haven't made time for her this week. Things do not, typically, come out of nowhere. There are two sides to every story, or more accurately, rarely is there one single story.

Whilst this used to irritate me (still does, in fact, for who doesn't want their mum to be their biggest cheerleader?), I know in some base place that she is right. When I zoom out of my own small world and look at things a bit more broadly, it is clear that the single story will always be inadequate. More than inadequate, it is dangerous. In her 2009 TED Talk, novelist Chimamanda Ngozi Adichie spoke about this, explaining that the single story is dangerous because it "creates stereotypes, and the problem with stereotypes is not that they are untrue, but that they are incomplete."[1] Many of us are guilty of either creating or upholding stereotypes in some way or another: assumptions we make about people based on the way they vote, the way they eat, the music they like, and the clothes they wear. Stereotypes help us code and place and make sense. This is not necessarily harmful; it is just a part of what it is to be a human, coexisting with others who are like us but are not us and trying to understand where we fit. However, while stereotypes do not have to be harmful, they are by nature reductive. And the word "reductive" is very telling: It reduces, makes less. Reducing anything or anyone to less than their whole inevitably has an ugly side. The particularly ugly side as far as stereotypes are concerned is that the stereotypes that really stick, those that have the greatest authority, are the ones that are held and enforced by those in society (or in any group) who are more powerfully positioned. And Adichie is right: They are not always entirely untrue. Often they start from a place of some logic. They begin based on observations that might have applied to a certain group of people at a certain time. But inevitably, they end up placing some groups of people in tight boxes, whilst others have the freedom to stand on top of the boxes and jump about, moving from box to box as and when they wish. Black women are up there with the groups that society has loved, more than almost all others, to shut away and seal the lid.

Despite this, there are examples of Black women throughout history who have refused to be put into a box or to be relegated to a single lane. They have stood their ground, followed their heart, and said *no*. They have unapologetically changed the single-handed and reductive narrative, rejecting the single story and allowing us, their descendants, to breathe in the scent of choice—and of freedom.

One woman who embodies this spirit of blazing her own path and defying the single story is Hattie McDaniel: actress, activist, and pioneer, a woman who was truly ahead of her time. In February 1940, dressed in a turquoise gown studded with rhinestones and with white gardenias (her favorite flower) in her hair, Hattie McDaniel made her way from a small table set against a wall where she was segregated at the back of the 12th Academy Awards to the stage to accept the Best Supporting Actress Oscar. Awarded for playing Mammy in the cultural classic *Gone with the Wind*, McDaniel was the first Black person in history to win such an award. The next Black woman to receive the honor was Whoopi Goldberg, some fifty-one years later. In 2002, Halle Berry became the first Black woman to receive the Oscar for Best Actress in a Leading Role, after seventy-three years of awards ceremonies. No Black woman has won the award for Best Actress in the two decades since. Despite the 2023 joy of Michelle Yeoh's euphoric victory as the first Asian woman to win Best Actress in a Leading Role, as of the 95th Academy Awards, only thirty-eight Oscars have been awarded to actors from global majority backgrounds.

Bleak. And possibly more bleak is that after the euphoria of the moment that Halle Berry won, from her speech in which she publicly honored every "nameless, faceless woman of color that now has a chance because this door tonight has been opened," it feels in many ways like nothing has changed. Black women are still jostling for their seat at the table. And yet, maybe we can focus on the progress that has been made, take inspiration from the single story that was shattered on that day in 1940 when the woman with white gardenias in her hair made history.

What I am interested in is how a Black woman from Kansas ended up being the first person in the history of her race to win this coveted honor in the first place. One thing I am sure of is that McDaniel was born to be a performer. The youngest of thirteen children, she decided to become an actress at the age of six. She was so obsessed with performing that her mother would sometimes pay her a nickel just to get her to stop singing and dancing at all times. McDaniel couldn't be stopped, though. In May 1914, aged almost twenty-one, after a childhood working in traditional vaudeville and minstrel shows, including those of her brother Otis McDaniel, Hattie and her sister Etta decided to put on their own productions. Their first significant endeavor was an all-female minstrel show. Named the McDaniel Sisters Company, the collective performed as a fundraiser for a local women's organization and went on to have a regular slot in their Denver hometown, gaining popularity and respect as they went and technically becoming the first Black female producers on record. With every performance, McDaniel stepped further away from the stereotypes surrounding race and gender at the time, even turning them on their head by performing in "whiteface." Typically, women didn't act onstage in the early twentieth century, especially Black women and especially in shows that were intelligent and witty and took to task racial and gendered social norms. McDaniel was out to change that. Even down to the master of ceremonies, every key role in McDaniel's shows was played by a woman. She would famously make the all-Black audience roar with laughter as she faced the Mammy figure head-on and showcased it for what it really was: a grotesque extreme. She began to be hugely respected in Denver's Black community, a force to be reckoned with who was totally in command and at home onstage. Born a poor Black child to two formerly enslaved—and poverty-stricken—people, according to the traditional single story McDaniel was destined to live one type of life. Instead, she found a platform she could stand on, breaking out of her box to have a clear and determined voice.

At the age of twenty-one, McDaniel became a widow, suddenly losing her husband to pneumonia. Her brother Otis died around the same time and the McDaniel Sisters Company was disbanded shortly after. McDaniel moved around, singing the blues and working as a maid before beginning to act in some stage shows and finding a way to maintain her footing in an unstable world. Then, in 1929, the tentative stability she had found was torn out from beneath her. McDaniel had been performing in Milwaukee in the musical *Show Boat* when the financial crash forced the show to close, leaving her destitute. Never one to be kept down and out, though, she found a job working in the toilets at a white nightclub for around seven dollars a week—in her mind ever preferable to the alternative work as a maid facing her at the time. Resiliently, she put up with this for some months until, out of nowhere, the remarkable happened. As McDaniel told the story, she had gone to work at the nightclub as usual, but the headline act hadn't shown up and the club's band was left without a singer. McDaniel stepped forward and sang out a version of "St. Louis Blues," which (obviously) brought the house down. She was hired as a singer on the spot. Her next stop, at the age of thirty-eight, was Hollywood.

In May 1931, McDaniel started working as a film extra. The work was unpredictable and often demeaning (requiring

McDaniel to play stereotypical roles such as mammies and maids), but it still paid better—and fed McDaniel's creativity far more—than the alternative of actually being a maid ever would. "I'd rather play a maid than be one,"[2] she was particularly fond of saying. Or, the especially satisfying: "I'd rather play a maid and make $700 a week than be a maid and make $7."[3] Whilst this was radical and even inspiring, it also trod somewhat delicate ground, given what the majority of her contemporaries were doing for work. Despite her seeming resolve and the obvious financial incentives, playing a maid brought with it a whole wave of difficulties and compromises. McDaniel was suddenly playing the very parts that she had spent her earlier years mocking and criticizing as the leader of her Sisters Company. Well aware of this, she started fighting back. Using subtle gestures such as her body language or tone of voice, McDaniel would push against the tired image of the docile, loving Black servant woman. White audiences found this hilarious, lapping up seeing her rolling her eyes or sucking her teeth, but what they didn't realize was that this was not just "comedy gold." It was calculated and it was real. It was McDaniel's own inside joke, a middle finger up to the single story that reduced her to less than she was prepared to be.

By late 1935, McDaniel was a recognized face in the film industry. She regularly received speaking roles and was becoming more frequently credited for them both on-screen and in the press. She had worked for almost all of the well-known Hollywood studios and with many of the stars of the day. She counted actors such as Clark Gable among her closest friends. After she landed the leading role of Queenie in Universal's much-anticipated film adaptation of *Show Boat*, which went on to become a box-office success, McDaniel's career entered another level.

Working steadily, McDaniel began to be able to support her family financially—unprecedented territory for the youngest daughter in a long line of boys. She purchased her first house. Her charitable works were important to her too, ranging from the Red Cross relief programs for Americans who had been displaced by the 1937 Ohio River floods (many of whom were Black) to becoming a figurehead for a number of fundraising efforts with the goal of advancing the lives of African-American people. By supporting efforts such as Delta Sigma Theta's scholarship fund for young Black women wishing to attend college, she grew a reputation within the Black community as someone who was unquestioningly generous.

Off-screen, she worked hard to distance herself from the servile parts that she had become synonymous with by dressing in the latest fashions and showcasing her beauty. She hosted iconic parties in her seventeen-room mansion, where the biggest stars would come together irrespective of color, McDaniel the epitome of an ever-glamorous host with her beloved Dalmatians by her side. On-screen, however, while continuing to make a point of infusing each role with defiance and with her trademark disdainful glare, McDaniel was still playing maids. She observed to her friend, actress Lena Horne:

"I'm a fine Mammy [on the screen]. But I'm Hattie McDaniel in my house."[4] McDaniel knew—and to some extent probably resented—that despite her success, in the eyes of mainstream America she was still imprisoned in her box, shackled within a single story that spoke only to a racist vision of Black America and refused to see Black women in any other way.

Things were not any easier for McDaniel within the Black community, and calls began to grow for Hollywood to end the damaging stereotypes of "Blackness." Black actors were frequently on the receiving end of this criticism: If they just stopped playing these roles then the parts would stop existing. Or so the thinking went. For McDaniel, however, things were not that straightforward. Performing was her livelihood; but more than that, she felt that she was navigating the small-mindedness of Hollywood in as respectful a way as she possibly could—and making small inroads in its racist perceptions along the way. In her eyes, she was on the right side of history. Because of this, the demands from the Black community were both isolating and insulting. Aware that if she sided with the Black community she would risk her career, and yet if she sided with Hollywood she would alienate her own people, McDaniel opted for silence and refused to make any public statements, in the belief that she could both preserve her career and be a passionate advocate for the racial advancement of Black people—a near impossible task that was about to get harder, for it was the very next year that McDaniel would face her biggest challenge yet.

Gone with the Wind, a novel published in 1936 by Margaret Mitchell, at that point an unknown Southern journalist, was controversial right from the start. Even before its publication, it had created such a stir that it had already captured Hollywood's attention. Producer David O. Selznick had paid an unprecedented $50,000 for the rights and the Black community made no secret of their disgust at this, reacting with immediate alarm mainly due to the book's harmful depiction of its Black characters. It used heavily racist stereotypes, referring to the Ku Klux Klan as a "tragic necessity," repeatedly using the N-word, infantilizing or, worse, dehumanizing its Black characters, and, like many works of the time, viewed slavery through rose-tinted glasses. While protests raged around her, the quietly considerate McDaniel bought the book and decided to read it for herself.

The casting process for the film was a nationwide search that went on for more than a year and even involved First Lady Eleanor Roosevelt submitting her own maid. Eventually, at forty-five years old, McDaniel triumphed, securing her highest profile role yet: She was going to play Mammy in the biggest film of the year. By this point the criticism from the Black community had reached extreme levels and she was widely viewed as having sold out. Earl J. Morris, motion picture editor of the *Pittsburgh Courier*, wrote of her new role that: "It means about $2,000 for Miss McDaniel in individual advancement . . . [and] nothing in racial advancement," even going so far as to equate Black participation in the film to "racial suicide."[5]

In the white community, things were far from smooth sailing. Margaret Mitchell responded to the growing protests and criticism from the Black community by stating that she did "not intend to let any trouble-making Professional Negros" influence her.[6] David O. Selznick's thoughts were a little more complex, perhaps recognizing that the world was (slowly) changing. Writing to screenwriter Sidney Howard, he stated that: "I for one have no desire to produce any anti-Negro film. In our picture I think we have to be awfully careful that the Negroes come out decidedly on the right side of the ledger."[7] He worked hard to omit some of the most offensive material in the book, such as removing references to the Ku Klux Klan and lynchings. Black villains in the novel were transformed into white ones for the film. However, Selznick famously fought hard to keep the N-word in the script for reasons of historical accuracy.

Hundreds of letters of protest continued to be sent in to the production company. Selznick launched a publicity offensive, hoping to charm the Black press and quell the protests. But still, the N-word remained, with Selznick stating that he could not "believe that we would offend any Negroes if we use the [N-word] with care."[8] However, some weeks later, seemingly without any explanation, Selznick ordered it to be dropped from the script. The fact that this word, which was due to have been spoken by Mammy, never made it on-screen led many to speculate whether McDaniel herself had played a role in this by refusing to utter the word.

She never claimed credit for this publicly. Perhaps this was part of her mission to remain palatable to white Hollywood. Hollywood's PR machine was certainly keen to promote McDaniel's "respectability" and went into overdrive as it sought to build tight walls around her, protecting its investment by placing a single story within a single box. McDaniel used to say that she was always acting and playing a part, blurring the lines of reality and fiction as she refused to be defined. While trying not to alienate her Black critics, this also meant that she had to be willing to do anything to survive in white Hollywood, even if it meant situating herself within a box that was not of her making. She charmed the studio executives by boasting about her experiences as a cook and bringing in home-baked treats for them. This was the sort of thing that the producers lapped up, using it to paint a narrative in the media of McDaniel and her Mammy character as being intertwined. They would emphasize her early years trying to break through in Hollywood whilst working as a maid and downplay the "unpalatable" aspects, such as her time as a blues singer. The creation of the single story extended to her family, too. Her father became a Baptist preacher and not the man who fled slavery to fight against the very people put on a pedestal in *Gone with the Wind*. McDaniel was represented as cheerful, hardworking, compliant, and completely unthreatening to the dominant social order. These sorts of stories were reproduced in the press—a Mammy playing a Mammy—and

McDaniel did nothing to dissuade anyone from thinking they were true. These were her coping tactics. This was survival.

This all became a part of her performance, too. She would channel those early years in Denver, when she would revel in showing sheer disdain in her minstrel shows and her great fiery independence in singing the blues. Mammy was infused with the complexities of a living, breathing woman. In short, McDaniel brought herself—all of herself—to the role, just not in the way that the studios were suggesting. The effect of this became obvious when the producers reviewed the final cut of the film: McDaniel leaped off the screen. Predicting that the world was about to witness the birth of a star, Selznick signed her immediately to an exclusive long-term contract before anyone else could beat him to it.

The hype was so great for the film's release that the day of the premiere was declared a statewide holiday in Georgia. As ever, though, things were not straightforward, even for the next big star. Because of the Jim Crow laws in place forbidding Black and white people from mixing, McDaniel and the rest of the Black cast were not allowed to attend the Atlanta premiere. Their headshots were not even allowed to be included next to those of the white actors in the program for the film and, in a misguided attempt to compromise, were eventually removed altogether. McDaniel's performance, filled with subtlety, defiance, and heavy emotional complexity, brought the house down. If you look closely, there are barely noticeable signs in her costume too that McDaniel was bringing to life Mammy as we had never seen her before. She wore large, expensive-looking rings and had beautifully manicured nails—understated signals that this was a woman who took pride in herself, a woman who did not and could not possibly put the white family she worked for above herself. It was one of the few times in history that a Black actor had been given the opportunity to bring to life a character with any sort of emotional depth behind them.

Margaret Mitchell wrote to McDaniel after the Atlanta premiere that she had been banned from: "I wish you could have heard the applause."[9] This statement breaks my heart: the injustice that McDaniel was not allowed to hear the applause that so rightly should have elevated her soul. Columnist and radio personality Jimmie Fidler clearly felt the same, believing that despite everything, Hollywood would never give McDaniel the opportunities she deserved. Speaking of the sad but inevitable truth that she would go back to playing comedy maids, he said: "I don't think it will be easy for me to laugh at Hattie's comedy in the future for I'll never be able to overlook the tragic fact that a very great artist is being wasted."[10] What a tragedy that even in the face of one of the truly great performances of its time, this courting of the single story by the Hollywood PR machine meant that McDaniel would seemingly still never be permitted to break out of her box.

Meanwhile, Black Americans protested outside the cinemas in huge numbers, with signs such as: YOU'D BE SWEET TOO

UNDER A WHIP and "GONE WITH THE WIND" HANGS THE FREE NEGRO. Walter White, leader of the civil rights organization the National Association for the Advancement of Colored People (NAACP), spoke out, asking Black actors to stop "mugging and playing the clown before the camera."[11] While not directed straight at McDaniel, White made no secret of his disapproval of her career choices. In response, McDaniel, who had mostly opted for a dignified silence, finally spoke out. She stated that she had based her interpretation of Mammy not on a racist creation of white imaginations but instead on the strongest women of the era: Harriet Tubman, Sojourner Truth, and Charity Still—abolitionists. Heroines. In words that send a shiver down my spine, she declared that Mammy's legacy was not determined by the white people she served (as the Hollywood PR machine would have had the world believe) but instead by "the brave efficient type of womanhood which, building a race, mothered Booker T. Washington, George Carver, Robert Moton, and Mary McLeod Bethune."[12] In a blazing display of power, McDaniel shared with the world her own reasoning for why she agreed to play Mammy: "This is an opportunity to glorify Negro womanhood. I am proud that I am a Negro woman because members of that class have given so much."[13]

Different words, but McDaniel was recognizing the golden thread connecting her irrevocably to those who had come before. And, looping full circle back to where we began, on February 29, 1940, she also recognized those who would come after. McDaniel was nominated for an Oscar, the highest accolade an actor could wish for. After she was initially banned from attending the ceremony, Selznick called in a favor to persuade the venue to make an exception to its strict "no Blacks" policy, and on the condition that she sit at a segregated table in the back of the room, entirely separate from her white co-stars, McDaniel was allowed to attend the 12th Academy Awards.

Sat in my room, hunched over my laptop, watching the clip of McDaniel walking onstage, the only Black woman amid a sea of white faces, to collect her award for Best Actress in a Supporting Role, is a moving experience. So visibly overcome that she can barely hold back her tears, McDaniel faces the audience and addresses them:

> *This is one of the happiest moments of my life. . . . Thank you . . . for your kindness. It has made me feel very, very humble and I shall always hold it as a beacon for anything that I may be able to do in the future. I sincerely hope I shall always be a credit to my race and to the motion picture industry. My heart is too full to tell you just how I feel, and may I say thank you and God bless you.*[14]

Hattie McDaniel, the daughter of enslaved people, was collecting the highest honor in Hollywood. She sobs, and I am weeping for her and with her. Her comment to reporters on the way out? "I did my best and God did the rest."[15] The next morning she was on the front of every single paper.

According to IMDb, adjusted for inflation, *Gone with the Wind* is still the highest-grossing film of all time. In June 2020 it was temporarily removed from HBO Max, in the wake of the resurgence of the Black Lives Matter movement. This acknowledgment that a racial reckoning was needed only further serves to prove the point that this film is a part of the American cultural consciousness—and is being taken seriously. It matters.

McDaniel wrote a think piece for a 1947 edition of *The Hollywood Reporter* and one line in it sticks out to me, singing my name: "I have never apologized for the roles I play."[16] I read this sentence again and again, weaving it into my own understanding of a woman who lived a hundred years before me. I love it. I love it with my whole heart. *I have never apologized . . .* In that one sentence, McDaniel not only speaks out against her critics, but she does so with such eloquence and passion that hers can be nothing but the final word. You get the sense that far from her apologizing to anyone, it is the world who should be apologizing to her. In a dignified but blazing response to all who spoke out against her, McDaniel writes of how "people are always telling me about the 'lucky break' I got in pictures. I don't take the trouble to tell them of all the years I sang in choruses, worked in mob scenes, thankful for the smallest thing. A call from Charlie Butler at Central Casting was like a letter from home, a bit part with a line of dialogue was like manna from heaven."[17] As an actor myself, well used to the grind of putting yourself through audition after audition and the innumerable rejections that accompany every "yes," this resonates. It is perhaps why I celebrate every victory, no matter how small. I've fought for everything that I've achieved. I haven't gotten lucky. I work hard and I am getting what I deserve.

This summarizes precisely how I felt rewatching *Gone with the Wind* for the first time after viewing McDaniel's Oscar acceptance speech. This is a woman who continuously and relentlessly played mammies. She played maids. She played sexless, loveless individuals whose sole function was to reinforce white Southern romanticism. What people don't know is that McDaniel was married four times. She was sexy, a sex symbol to many. This sits firmly at odds with the single story—the desexualized image of the Mammy the world would like us to see. One of my favorite photos of McDaniel is an iconic picture of her standing by a fireplace wearing a fur coat. It reminds me of when Aretha Franklin came out for that cataclysmic performance at the Kennedy Center Honors and sang "(You Make Me Feel Like) A Natural Woman" in front of the Obamas and Carole King. Michelle Obama was singing along. The president of the United States of America was wiping away his tears. Carole King was on her feet, crying and screaming and looking around in disbelief at the "Queen of Soul" singing her song. The entire Kennedy Center got to their feet and it was all for Aretha. A woman, a natural woman. Every single inch of her. Just thinking about it makes me swell with joy. This was a woman who was in her prime.

She was seventy-three years old, dressed in a fur coat, and as she ripped it off and flung it to the floor at the emotional climax, there had never been anyone sexier. She was pride and power and talent and strength—all traits that McDaniel had in bucketloads. These women were fashionistas. They were icons. They were lusted after, idolized, and adored.

Why, then, does the single story not let us see this? Why has McDaniel until recently been ostracized from both the white and the Black cultural consciousness? Even when the late great Sidney Poitier passed away in January 2022, my social media accounts were flooded with people honoring the "first Black person to win an Oscar," something that is just palpably untrue. McDaniel was first by some twenty-four years. Of course, much of this comes down to the simple fact that she was a woman, but I can't help feeling that it must be more complex than that. Many people since, including author Pearl Cleage, have simply said that they were too radical to appreciate McDaniel's genius.[18] It was drilled into them to be judgmental of her, angry even, because she won the Oscar for playing a character who was supposedly demeaning to Black people everywhere. Whilst of course this is true, I am struck by how little interest in the real person behind the character it shows. Actress Mo'Nique (who seventy years after McDaniel's win dressed in the same turquoise dress with white gardenias in her hair to accept her own Academy Award in honor of her predecessor) states: "That woman had to endure questions from the white community *and* the Black community.

But she said, 'I'm an actress—and when you say, "Cut," I'm no longer that.' If anybody knew who this woman really was, they would say, 'Let me shut my mouth.'"[19] McDaniel was not subservient. She refused to be, and it pains me that people didn't look close enough to see that at the time. In not recognizing this, we all miss out. It was McDaniel's refusal to be neatly categorized and to adhere to the single story that made her fall out of favor with many whilst simultaneously being her biggest reclamation. It was her defiance.

To me, McDaniel's lasting legacy is obvious. She is an Oscar-winning actor. She was inducted into the Colorado Women's Hall of Fame, her face is on a postage stamp, and she has two stars on the Hollywood Walk of Fame. As well as her acting, there were her many blues singles, the fact that she was the first Black woman to sing on the radio in America, and that she appeared in over three hundred films (despite being officially credited for only eighty-three).

Delve even deeper into her life and you will see that her impact reaches far beyond cinema. In 1945, she played a pivotal role in desegregating housing in Los Angeles when some of the white residents in her neighborhood filed a lawsuit against the thirty-one Black residents. They cited a housing covenant that was in place and restricted certain demographics from buying in the area. McDaniel took personal control over this cause and organized Saturday workshops, eventually gathering two hundred and fifty supporters who went to court with her. They won the case, which went on to become a landmark ruling, setting a precedent that directly contributed, just three years later, to the Supreme Court ruling it unconstitutional for courts to enforce housing covenants.[20]

In her last days, as iconic as ever, McDaniel threw a death-bed party, welcoming all those who knew and loved her to come and join her for drinks and laughs. Guests would go in one or two at a time and say their goodbyes with the feeling, more than anything else, of celebrating the life she had led. In her last will and testament, McDaniel left detailed instructions for her funeral: "I desire a white casket and a white shroud; white gardenias in my hair and in my hands, together with a white gardenia blanket and a pillow of red roses."[21] She also wrote of her wish to be buried in Hollywood Cemetery, something that was denied due to its whites-only policy, a final betrayal from the Hollywood status quo. McDaniel knew she belonged there, though, and in 1999, her great-nephew Edgar Goff helped to achieve her final dream by successfully lobbying to get a marble memorial in her honor placed at the Hollywood Forever Cemetery, as it is known today. The epitaph calls back to those breathtaking words from her Oscar acceptance speech: "Aunt Hattie, you are a credit to your craft, your race and to your family."

These last wishes do not speak of a woman who was subservient in any way. What they do show is someone who knew precisely what she wanted and was instead pulled in multiple opposing directions by the world around her. Often, Black female power is played out in the middle of noise. It requires a juggling on the part of Black women, a navigation that involves seeing, hearing, and acknowledging the noise on both sides—in McDaniel's case from both her Black critics and the white powers that be, and then putting her best face forward and saying, *I know what I'm doing, I know who I am—and I am going to do it my way.* Why are Black women particularly adept at navigating the stereotypes that the world continues to place on them? Because we have a lifetime's experience of doing exactly that. And it is in this space in between one single story or the other that the barriers that hold us back are obliterated. We should recognize those who are brave enough to do so.[22]

In Hattie McDaniel's own words:

I have learned something worth far more,
Than victory brings to men,
Battered and beaten, bruised and sore,
I can still come back again
    . . .
Trained upon pain and punishment,
I've groped my way through the night,
But the flag still flies from my tent,
And I've only begun the fight.

—HATTIE McDANIEL[23]

And, as we know, she never, ever apologized.

Part II

RE-CREATION

*In which we explore Black women's innovation
in creating their situations anew*

Chapter Four

FORMATION

"FORMATION," BEYONCÉ'S 2016 ANTHEM that ricocheted across the world after her incendiary Super Bowl performance, sang out against police brutality, the government response to Hurricane Katrina, and the idea that Blackness is anything other than beautiful. It simultaneously elevated an unapologetic love for Black culture and, most important, the power of the collective, of a formation. Throughout the song, Beyoncé moves through time, class, and place as she invokes the different methods of Black resistance. There is the overt expression of deeds not words, familiar to many of us from the cries of the suffragettes. This resistance can look like anything from brandishing guns to staging coups to taking a physical stand. Next, there is the quiet, preparatory, and almost meditative kind of resistance—preparing for a battle of words and ideology. We see this on social media, in interviews, and on television shows. Then, there is "*formation*," an altogether different sort of resistance. *Formation* is the kind of resistance that places collective action and creativity right at its heart. Just as a dance troupe must get in perfect formation, for this sort of resistance to be successful, there must be total coordination. Black women, as they organize, strategize, move, and create, must get in formation. To do this—to truly create a perfect formation—no piece or person can be missing. Every single member—each contribution— matters and so the formation is also a metaphor for all of those at the intersection of Blackness and womanhood: queer, trans, nonbinary, working class, neurodiverse, disabled, immigrant—they all belong. They all contribute. They all matter. When you think of it like this, Beyoncé's "Formation" is a call to arms.

The vision of this formation of Black women, in perfect synchrony as they communicate across time, space, and situation, can be seen throughout history and especially in the collaboration of Black women in Europe, Africa, North America, and the Caribbean in the early twentieth century. Just like Beyoncé, these women used art, music, and the emergence of new forms of global media to create a literary and political resistance to the dominant narratives of their time about Blackness and womanhood. Women such as Claudia Jones, born in Trinidad and Tobago in 1915, went on to change the course of history. By the time she died in 1964— at the age of just forty-nine—Jones had transformed the face of the Black Power movement worldwide. After moving as a child from the Caribbean to the United States, she went on to become a communist political activist, feminist, and Black nationalist, which eventually led to her deportation during the McCarthy era's campaign against those on the political left. She ended up in the United Kingdom, where she founded the *West Indian Gazette*, Britain's first major Black newspaper, and, perhaps most significantly, played a central role in founding the Notting Hill Carnival, now the second-largest annual carnival in the world and a place where arts, culture, and a total celebration of Blackness meet and thrive. Jones defied definition and used her platform not only to advocate for fierce political change but also to promote unashamed self-love. Noticing that many beauty contests at the time were strictly reserved for white or extremely light-skinned Black people, Jones used the *West Indian Gazette* as a means of appealing to as many Caribbean people as possible and encouraging them to be proud of their identity and their beauty.

Across the Channel, Caribbean sisters Jeanne and Paulette Nardal had moved from Martinique to France, where they built a political resistance as writers and publishers. They used their language skills to push for cross-cultural communications, writing about everything from Afro-Latin identity to European fetishism of Black women and Black music in the United States.

By using their art to create meaningful connections across the globe, just as Beyoncé did in crafting her own formation a century later, Black women such as Jones and the Nardal sisters were able to carve out new spaces for their work. They established themselves as writers, activists, and pioneers— forces to be reckoned with. Their resistance was unique because it was two pronged. At a time when Black men were fighting racism and white women were battling sexism, Black women's resistance came from a rejection of both sexism and racism, a radical departure from all that had been seen before. It was a resistance made up of those who stood at a crossroads: race, class, gender—every individual standing at an intersection of society was welcome. In my mind, this looks very much like what we now know to be "intersectionality," a term coined by Professor Kimberlé Crenshaw in 1989 to refer to how the different elements of an individual's identity come together to establish both discrimination and privilege.

In fact, Claudia Jones's 1949 essay "An End to the Neglect of the Problems of the Negro Woman" actually helped to establish the foundations of intersectionality and feminism as we know them today. The resistance of these women was powerful because it was *inclusive*. It was inclusive because it was neither the overt bravado and spectacle of a physical resistance nor the subtle musings of an intelligentsia lost in libraries and private correspondence. Rather, this was a resistance born out of creativity and connection. As the Nardal sisters opened their literary salons in Paris in the 1920s to all who passed through, Claudia Jones was joining America's Young Communist League. Theirs was a shared resistance that took place in churches and in kitchens and was frequently overlooked. Just as you may not notice individual dancers as they perform a sequence, but rather marvel at the wonder of the collective, so has history blurred the names and faces of the individual Black women getting in formation. Millions of people celebrate Notting Hill Carnival each year, but how many know that its founding mother is a Black woman? How many know that she played a part not only in fighting for racial equality in the UK, but in bringing Caribbean culture to the forefront of British life? How many people know that she was deported, arrested, and sentenced to prison four times,[1] or that she was responsible for the first televised Black beauty competition in the UK? How many people know that she dedicated her life to liberating her own Black people? Much of the societal progress that we see today, one example being the now deeply valued cultural institution that the Notting Hill Carnival has become, can be traced back to the work of our foremothers. Their resistance—their formation—used creativity and connections to lift those who came after them.

At the turn of the twentieth century, Black women were at the heart of instigating dynamic social change. The world around them was shifting rapidly, marking a moment of modernity and internationalism. New forms of mass media, travel, and globalization were coming together to create a more interconnected world, and Black women were right at the center of these changes, creating opportunities for themselves and their descendants. Septima Poinsette Clark, fondly referred to as the "queen mother" of the civil rights movement, created citizenship schools that helped enfranchise and empower African Americans. American-born French entertainer, French Resistance agent, and civil rights activist Josephine Baker epitomized Black American beauty whilst doubling up as a spy in the Second World War. From Jones to Poinsette Clark to Baker, Black women were creating new spaces for themselves and writing themselves back into the stories that they had been excluded from, before passing the mantle down to their daughters to do the same.

Just as with the freedwomen breathing new life into the Mammy figure, one of these spaces is the kitchen. By asserting their authority in these sacred spaces where they have total control, Black women have been able to use cooking as a means of transcending social boundaries. Going as far back as the nineteenth century, the formerly enslaved Malinda Russell, author of the earliest known cookbook by a Black woman, not only published her recipes but went on to earn her living as a cook. With recipes for items such as floating island, puff pastry, and rose cake, Russell's cookbook is extraordinary in painting a picture of Black cuisine as sophisticated and elaborate, a blending of cosmopolitan ingredients and intriguing flavors for the sake of sheer delight rather than simply for sustenance. Russell's race and gender should have made her invisible in the early nineteenth century, and at a time when many of her contemporaries were enslaved people, her entrepreneurship is even more striking. For Russell to publish a cookbook at that time took gumption and audacity. She dared to envision a future where Black women could create—and they could do so with confidence. Seeing her creativity as part of a global movement of Black women getting in formation is exciting because it begins to teach us a little about the historical legacy—the thread of gold—that Black women have left in recipes, cookbooks, and family secrets. One of the few pieces of information that we do know about Malinda Russell is that she had a disabled son and was raising him alone after her husband died. In publishing her cookbook, she hoped to earn enough money for their passage back home to Tennessee, where she had successfully run a boardinghouse and a pastry shop for eight years before fleeing to Michigan after a brutal robbery. One of the most remarkable things about Russell's cookbook for me is her clear determination to honor the women who came before her. She describes how she was taught to cook by Fanny Steward, a Black cook whose name would otherwise have faded into obscurity with the passing of time. This makes me think not only of Malinda and Fanny, but of all the other Black women weaving this thread whose names we may never know. Their work was not deemed of worth and yet for Malinda Russell, and for so many of these women, creativity through cooking was a display of both personal resilience and political resistance in all their glory. Too often we have focused on driving women out of the kitchen because it is traditionally associated with oppression, domesticity, and housekeeping. This ignores the legacy of the women, like Malinda Russell, who have forged groundbreaking paths in these spaces. These women have used food both as an act of resistance and as a way of creating something new—constructing their identities and telling their own stories.

Identity construction as a Black woman is a difficult and sometimes painful process, and I am no stranger to how lonely it can feel when you try to go it alone. There is no blueprint for who we are. Our history isn't typically taught to us in school, or at least not beyond the bloody and demeaning history of slavery. I certainly didn't grow up seeing an empowering past on television or in the books I read—and believe me, I searched. Searching was precisely what I was doing during the summer I discovered a book that would change my perspective and everything I had previously thought about what it meant to be a young Black woman.

It was toward the end of my stay at Jacqueline's when I stumbled across French-Caribbean writer Maryse Condé's *Victoire: My Mother's Mother* (translated from the French *Victoire, les saveurs et les mots*). I was looking for a book that I could read in French that would connect me with Guadeloupe during the rest of my time there before I headed farther afield to Martinique, to Saint Lucia, Saint Martin, and, finally, the motherland—Jamaica. I wanted to connect, somehow, with my mother and with the world she came from. This was where I found myself when I picked up *Victoire* for the first time. Ostensibly on the trip of a lifetime, I hopped from island to island seeking the answers to my past and therefore to my future. I went to the Caribbean expecting to reclaim something fundamental to my sense of self—to fill in the missing pieces in the puzzle of my life, to belong and feel instantly at home. It wasn't as straightforward as that. While I felt as though I belonged on a superficial level—I taught myself Créole, my skin was golden, and I spent my evenings dancing on a tropical island under the stars—there was something missing: As far as the Guadeloupeans were concerned, I didn't belong. I was a British girl in the Caribbean. An English tourist, holidaying in a place that was not, and would never be, mine. This felt like the ultimate rejection. If I couldn't belong in Britain, the place of my birth, and I was such an obvious outsider in the Caribbean, the islands I came from, then where did that leave me? Where did I fit into this story? Who was I?

It was on arrival in Jamaica that I began, finally, to address some of these questions and discover the many women—my ancestors—who had been asking themselves these questions and seeking the answers in any way they could since time immemorial. For me, as with so many women who came before me, the answer came through cooking. After I left Jacqueline's in Guadeloupe and island-hopped a little on my own, my sister Laura came out to meet me and we finally ended up in Jamaica, staying with our aunt Eseen, a half sister of my mother who I had met once as a little girl. After weeks of solo traveling and never feeling truly comfortable, moving in with

Eseen with Laura by my side finally meant that I began to feel that I had permission to belong in this place, that it was rightfully a part of me. On our very first evening there she took us to the supermarket, introducing us to jackfruit and "pears" (avocados). She woke us the next morning with fried dumplings and ackee, something I was used to from big family Christmas breakfasts where forty of us crammed into a two-up two-down in Newport, South Wales, laughing and eating and arguing. "Auntie," I asked her after a few days, "do you think you might teach me to cook like a Jamaican?" She was pleased, I think, as she was to share anything about her home and our history. And so began our morning cookery lessons, with me feeling closer to my mother in a fundamental and new way by connecting with the sister she hardly knew. And little by little, along the way, I began to understand more about myself. After some weeks, finally, I pulled *Victoire* out of my suitcase and began reading.

Victoire's life is the perfect example of how one woman used food to create new possibilities and single-handedly change the narrative. Set at the turn of the twentieth century, *Victoire* is Condé's historical novel based on the true story of her grandmother's difficult life in Guadeloupe. Described by the narrator (Condé herself) as "a prisoner of her illiteracy, her illegitimacy, her gender," Victoire Elodie Quidal endures many hardships. She is biracial, almost white. Her mother was raped by a white man at the age of fourteen and died whilst giving birth to her. "God, how our mothers die young!"

Condé exclaims, cutting straight to the core of me as I thought of the many Black women still dying in childbirth for reasons that make no sense in the twenty-first century. After the death of her mother, Victoire was raised by her maternal grandmother, just as my own mother was raised by her grandmother in Jamaica after her parents left to try to make a better life for themselves in the United Kingdom. The life that Victoire goes on to lead is simultaneously so remarkable and so utterly ordinary that it can only be considered as nothing short of exceptional. Victoire never learned to read or write. She never learned to speak French, rendering her mute among Guadeloupe's burgeoning Black bourgeoisie. Eventually, she got herself a job where, in the words of her granddaughter, she was treated like a slave. Without pay, she started her work at six every morning and ended her day at seven or even eight at night. She wore her first pair of shoes when she was almost sixteen. And yet, pointing to the extraordinary nature of this ordinary story, she taught herself how to survive. Victoire taught herself to cook. Joining the collective of the alchemists who came before her, she wove a thread that became a life raft. Victoire defied definition, and when she fell pregnant, she knew that she would sacrifice everything—even herself— to make life better for her daughter.

Eventually, this is precisely what she did. She worked hard and was taken on as a servant and a cook by a white Creole family, where her talent for cooking brought her to the attention of prominent white Creoles. Eventually, even with her meager resources, she managed to open the doors of the up-per classes (known as "*les Grandes Nègres*") for her daughter—a space that she herself could never have hoped to occupy. On May 19, 1906, Victoire's daughter, Jeanne, was the first Black girl to pass her exams with the commendation of "excellent," which gave her access to the boarding school in Versailles, France, that she desperately wished to attend. When Jeanne passed her final high school exam, the newspaper *Le Nouvelliste* celebrated her success with a vibrant article headlined: ONWARD, NEGRESS! FORGE AHEAD!

The whole book for me was just the most exhilarating and complex mix of Caribbean culture, Black history, and ordinary women's lives. I felt both comforted and excited by the fact that Victoire, one hundred years earlier, had also tried to write her story, to fill in the gaps in her existence by exploring both cooking and writing. I considered for the first time that cooking could be an act of creative resistance. I realized that I had never before seen it treated as worthy of such respect—of any respect at all. Through Condé's eyes, I was able to see Victoire as a pioneer, using creativity in cooking to lift herself out of hardship; an acerbic act of self-definition from a woman who legally did not even possess her own surname. Most remarkable of all is that this woman who lived over one hundred years before me in a tiny village on a tiny island ensured that she left a legacy. She joined the collective of women using their resources, creativity, and passion to weave their story into the tapestry and make their mark on the world—in any way that they could. Writing a story is the way in which it is memorialized. It is the way in which we preserve it, declaring that it matters for those who come after us. Of course, this has been achieved in other ways for those without the ability to write, usually orally. But for servants such as Victoire, who could they tell their story to? Who would care to memorialize it? Who would even care to listen? Victoire wrote her story in her own way, carving out a space of domestic resistance in the face of oppression and hardship, through cooking.

The deceptively simple descriptions of Victoire at work are extraordinary in the picture that they paint. Victoire spent most of her time "locked in her temple of a kitchen . . . absorbed over her kitchen range like a writer hunched over her computer." I loved this drawing of an explicit parallel between cooking and writing. Who was she writing for? I wondered. The more I read the more I discovered the complexity of her resistance. Victoire was not writing for white people. Her cooking was her private, and deeply personal, act. Cooking for Victoire was an assertion of talent, personality, and ultimately, it was an act of love for her daughter. Just like Malinda Russell with her son, Victoire was on a one-woman mission to create a better life for her girl. This was the story she was writing—the formation she was getting in. Condé describes her sadness at the times when her daughter lost her appetite: "Since Jeanne ate nothing or very little, there was no cooking to be done . . . Such a situation is comparable to that of a writer who . . . is kept from her computer. What torture.

How does she fight that terrible feeling of uselessness that assails her?"

Somewhere deep in Victoire's pot, she had to find the reserves to throw even more imagination and creativity into her work: to cook for her daughter even when her daughter did not want to eat. Again, I thought of my own mother, waking up before the rest of the family to ensure that we had the breakfast we needed before we went about our day. I thought of her, tight-lipped, cutting half a grapefruit into minuscule pieces for me each morning before school, not satisfied until I had eaten every last morsel, when I decided I was too fat to eat breakfast in my teenage years. I thought of her adopting a whole new cuisine and language when I decided to become a vegetarian at the age of seven. She didn't try to talk me out of it; she just set to work in making sure that this was a sustainable and healthy option for a growing child. I thought of the weddings, the birthdays, and the funerals where, at the highest and the lowest of moments, my mother, my aunties, and my grandmother would be found in the kitchen singing or laughing or crying as, in perfect synchrony, they got in formation and cooked up a storm. My grandmother, alongside some of the "sisters" from her church, has spent the best part of a century helping those in need, cooking for her community. Was this resistance? I certainly had never considered it as such. And yet, it was—is—their domain, their world. It is a space where they are in total control. They are a tower of strength, of collaboration, and of creative flair. It doesn't matter what the world thinks of them in this space. They are in their element. They are queens and they reign supreme. Anything is possible.

Seeing cooking as a form of power—and a creative power at that—is revelatory because it changes the rules. It draws the parameters of a new world—an alternative universe where a Black woman who knows what she wants and can freely experiment with how she will get there is not difficult, aggressive, or troublemaking. She is informed, authoritative, and empowered, shining with her own determination. Condé even said of Victoire that "cooking was her Père Labat rum, her ganja, her crack, her ecstasy. She dominated the world. For a time she became God . . . like a writer." Drawing parallels between the cook and a writer and the cook and God is exciting for a number of reasons, not least being that in all the incarnations of God that I have come across, imagining Her as a Black woman cooking up a storm in the kitchen is a most remarkable rewriting of the well-trodden narrative.

And yet, we live in the world that we live in. Despite the fact that he grew up in the Middle East, Jesus Christ (in every incarnation I have seen) is portrayed as a white man. Accordingly, despite Victoire ultimately succeeding in her overall goal of making a better life for her daughter, such a display of talent from a Black woman drew the wrong sort of attention to her along the way. Victoire was not perceived as a talented creative forging a path, even in her own mind. She was in servitude. Her creations belonged to others. And so, by default, did her cooking, her imagination. Time and time again throughout history, creativity and Blackness have been seen through a particular lens. The reality is that creativity is an active choice. People write, paint, make magic out of their own two hands because they want to—need to, even. People create because it makes them feel alive or helps them make some sense of their life. This could be Victoire choosing to use cooking to tell her story or it could be "Swing Low, Sweet Chariot" coming from the darkness of the plantation fields: a thing of beauty as a response to a life of hardship. However, the narrative that is peddled when it comes to creativity and Blackness does not reflect the reality. Instead, it reinforces a denigrated vision of Blackness where, for example, cooking is not skillful but rather improvisational. It comes from throwing things together without any talent or craft. It denotes a lack of intelligence.

We see this play out with—even contribute to the creation of—the stereotypes and images that persist and pervade our daily existence. Think about the narrative that surrounds Black success: Achievements of Black people are seen as a lucky genetic inheritance rather than the product of hard work, talent, and sheer determination. When white people excel—from athletes to philosophers to actors—we tend to celebrate them and their skill on an individual basis. We put them on pedestals. They become our heroes. When Black people succeed (and it is important to note that this applies to Black people of all genders and not just women, although

Black women are the most discredited), *we explain away their achievement.* We deny them the credit they are due. "Black people are such good singers," we cry when a Black person wins a televised national singing competition. "The Ethiopians are unbeatable. Black people are just better at running," we say between friends or privately think when a Black athlete is heralded as the fastest person in the world. "Positive discrimination," we say knowingly when a Black person is promoted to board level or when we see a multiracial family on a Christmas ad—totally ignoring the "positive discrimination" found in the nepotism that has blessed our politicians, actors, and almost every white-collar worker for the past few centuries. For Black people, creativity, skill, and talent are rarely seen as goals that have been fought for and worked toward, but rather as ad hoc, improvised, and almost random. In this pot of resistance, Black women are seasoning the former: Their creativity is their active choice. However, the dish that is being served up in restaurants is the latter. Gombo is called okra. Ackee is called vegan scrambled eggs. The most talented runners, singers, and tennis players are explained away. The Black women are shut out.

In 1970, Vertamae Smart-Grosvenor, an American culinary anthropologist and food writer, published her landmark book on this, *Vibration Cooking: or, the Travel Notes of a Geechee Girl.* In it, she preaches food's ability to nourish, to connect people, to traverse regional boundaries, to feel like home, to be a mode of self-expression, to be improvisational, and to tell stories. The book is written as a mix of narrative and recipes and Smart-Grosvenor refuses to oversimplify African-American cooking, as much of American society did at the time. Instead, she points out that it is just as skillful as any other cuisine. As I grappled with my cooking lessons in my aunt Eseen's kitchen, this book was a game changer for me. Her recipe for "so-called okra," pertinently titled "Name Calling," is especially relevant to any conversation about Black women's resistance and creativity, even today. She states:

> *If you are wondering how come I say so-called okra it is because the African name of okra is gombo. Just like so-called Negroes. We are Africans. Negroes only started when they got here. I am a Black woman. I am tired of people calling me out of my name. Okra must be sick of that mess too. So from now on call it like it is. Okra will be referred to in this book as gombo. Corn will be called maize and Negroes will be referred to as Black people.*[2]

It is time—past time, even—to start calling things as they are. Throughout history, work specifically pioneered by certain marginalized groups has been discredited or commandeered by those more powerfully positioned. We have to recognize Black women's creativity, intelligence, and skill for what it is. It is not simply improvisational. To view it as such lends itself to appropriation, for if there is no skill involved then there are no ownership rights. In Victoire's case, as far as the dominant narrative went, if there was no real skill to cooking, then whoever owned the cook owned the recipes. So, as Victoire's skill and talent brought her the attention she rightfully deserved, her social status meant that, paradoxically, she lost control. She was forced to immortalize the creativity of her recipes in writing, revealing sacred parts of herself that, perhaps, she was not prepared to reveal. The narrator describes how Victoire "reluctantly confided in Anne-Marie [her employer] the secrets of her culinary composition so that the latter could name them and have them printed. As with a writer whose editor decides the title, cover, and illustrations of her book, it was partly like being dispossessed of her creation. She would have preferred to keep it a secret."[3] Victoire created and constructed her own resistance to the bitterness of her life, but it was never really hers to keep.

To me, reading this at my aunt's kitchen table, I was crushed with the cruelty of it. While Victoire's creativity showed her pioneering her own conception of identity in her own space, being forced to translate it to the written form was the worst kind of appropriation. Her employer stole her recipes from her, the story of her life that she wrote for her baby. It was private and it was personal, a little piece of her forever taken. For me, directly after spending months on the French island of Guadeloupe, I was hit even harder, almost haunted, by one particular fact: Victoire spoke only Créole. She was illiterate and uneducated. She had never had an opportunity to learn French. Her recipes were created in her head in her language and her voice. Taking them from her own tongue and translating them into the foreign French felt like a theft, an abuse. It was an invasion or a colonization of what rightfully belonged to her. Even her private act of resistance was taken from her and appropriated. I wept for Victoire, Condé's mother's mother. I wept for my own mother. I wept for what was taken from us. And then, after a while, I got up and I started cooking.

I thought a lot about the link between cooking and writing in the days after reading *Victoire*, interspersing my own musings on my time in the Caribbean—testing patois and its lyricism in my mouth like a child trying olives for the first time—with tasting new foods, learning to cook fried dumplings and ackee and saltfish in my aunt's kitchen. She had a quiet, methodical way about her and I think she sensed that this suited me. As I became more confident in the kitchen I began to think about the other women writing the story of their lives. What other quietly radical motives underpinned ostensibly mundane acts? I imagined the intricacies of the lives of the cleaners saving for an education or the hairdressers building an empire. I began to question the alternative motives throughout history for actions that we have unquestioningly assumed simply fit the dominant discourse. Just as I had done with reimagining Aunt Jemima, and bringing to life the real women we only ever got to know as Mammy, I began to peer through the windows of ordinary Black women and into the big pot of resistance that they were cooking up.

It was becoming clear to me that for Black women, creativity is truly a double-edged sword. Cooking serves as both a means of liberation and a reason for oppression—perpetuating stereotypes about women and domesticity at the same time it provides them with a sacred space where they are God. Thinking more about the close relationship between creativity and theft was illuminating: Once Black women's creations are released into the world they are open to being taken because *Black women's work is not valued*. Staying in the early twentieth century, this is perfectly demonstrated by Afro-Martiniquais writers and sisters Paulette and Jeanne Nardal. Hosting literary salons in Paris, the sisters provided a space for students, politicians, and artists from all over the world (French colonies as well as African Americans visiting Paris) to connect and support each other's work. They directly furthered literary, political, and cultural movements by traveling back and forth across the Atlantic to Europe and America. In February 1928, Jeanne Nardal was among the few female founding members of *La Dépêche africaine*, the official bimonthly newspaper of the Committee for the Defense of the Interests of the Black Race. Paulette joined the staff in June of that same year. The journal would run on and off for four years and was one of the most popular Black newspapers of its time, printing twelve to fifteen thousand copies in 1929. In the October 1928 issue, Jeanne published an essay entitled *"Pantins exotiques"* ("Exotic Puppets"), which talked about Parisian fascination and exotification of Black women. One hundred years later, living in Paris myself, I read this as though it had been written that week. I felt more beautiful during my time as an adopted Parisian than I ever had in my life, but there was always a slightly uneasy feeling that the desire I was met with stemmed from something "other." Teenage boys in the school where I worked would hum Rihanna songs under their breath as I walked past. Grown men would follow me on the street. I was twenty years old, buoyed enough with the naivety of youth to feel confident that I would come to no harm but old enough to know that something wasn't right. Jeanne's references to exotification felt astutely observed and still alarmingly accurate. The sisters also founded a journal, *La Revue du monde noir/The Review of the Black World* (1931–1932), which became a key literary space for Négritude—a literary, cultural, and intellectual movement aimed at raising Black consciousness across Africa and its diaspora.

Négritude inspired the birth of many movements across the world, including Afro-Surrealism, Créolité in the Caribbean, and Black is Beautiful in the United States. Serving as the Nardals did not only as founders of the journal but also as editors and translators, their work and contribution to Black identity construction and consciousness was groundbreaking. One of the essays published in the journal, titled *"L'Éveil de la conscience de race"* ("The Awakening of Race Consciousness"), assessed the progress of racial awareness among Caribbean intellectuals. Their ideas on this are powerful. They do not advocate giving up their French identity or renouncing their Blackness but rather finding a halfway point and embracing both Afro-Caribbean and French cultures. I felt a connection between them and Victoire, who allowed her recipes to be translated to French despite her misgivings but ensured that she used her cooking to uplift her daughter and, significantly, never renounced her Creole identity. I also felt a connection between her and myself. Perhaps the answer wasn't in being either British or Jamaican, but in accepting both parts of myself in all their complexity.

However, as is all too often the case for Black women, their contribution to Négritude—their creation—was not theirs to keep. Now if we speak of Négritude at all, we speak of its founding fathers at the expense of the mothers who birthed it. Just as Victoire's creations were taken from her, Black women's contributions to Négritude have been enormously discredited. Google the term "Négritude" and you will find over and over again male writer, poet, and politician Aimé Césaire. The women have actually been referred to as "midwives," nothing more than assistants at its birth. In correspondence from the year 1960, Paulette Nardal complained bitterly of her and her sister's erasure from their own creation in favor of poets and politicians like Césaire, Léon Damas, and Léopold Senghor—all male. Nardal wrote that they "took up the ideas tossed out by us and expressed them with flash and brio." Not going down without a fight, she continued, "We were but women, real pioneers—let's say that we blazed the trail for them."[4]

It is unfathomable to me that the likes of the Nardal sisters still have not received their dues. How are we still treating them as the Mammy—as midwives, or assistants, raising white children or creating entire social movements with next to no credit or thanks before eventually being all but forgotten? These women blazed a trail for us. They used the changing space of the early twentieth century to fight for a creative resistance, constructing and reconstructing their identities in defiance of a society that would only ever see them as one thing. They were true pioneers: able to connect across time, space, and situation to speak directly to us today. They were—still are, even—an army of Black women, a movement, scorching into their path an incendiary resistance across the oceans and the ages as they stand together and get in formation. The power for us today is that we can then use this to create a more representative connection with an understanding of the Black female experience—our mothers' mothers' experiences, whether in literature, politics, fighting for justice, or even cooking up a storm in our kitchens.

Self-consciously engaging in spaces such as these is vital, and clearly time is up on viewing Black women as sitting around "assisting" and making cups of tea. It was the unison of Black women in these contexts, coming together across the difference to share ideas, that created the New Negro and

Négritude movements. If you take these facts to their logical conclusion, Black women co-created Black modernism. Why have they never been credited with this before? Why have they not been represented at all? Why are they absent from the history books and our news feeds? It is time to look at this forgotten part of history through the eyes of the women who created it.

This matters. Representation matters. Voices matter. How do we hear a story? Whose perspective do we hear it from? What does its translation do to its truth? Black women have always been appropriated, talked over, misrepresented, and mistranslated. They have not been seen as the neutral voice or starting point, even when the story in question is their own. This is played with by Condé in her inclusion of un-translated Creole in a book with a relatively mainstream target audience. I like to think of it as her own rebellion. Paulette Nardal also used translation to draw attention to the representation of race and gender across the Black diaspora. Her publications were always bilingual, and this is important, underlining her belief that any conversation about Black liberation had to have a global context. She attempted to balance the traditional demands of the educated Black woman whilst always seeking to represent those who could not speak for themselves, just as Claudia Jones sought to do. These women clearly worked on the understanding that no one is free until all are free.

Class and the power (or lack thereof) that accompanies it

should always be part of a conversation about representation. And yet, where Black women are concerned it is often ignored in favor of race and gender. I have reflected on this a lot in recent years with discussions surrounding the implications of coronavirus on the poorer parts of society raising questions about how we see class. A report from the Economic Policy Institute in June 2020 found that Black women were the least likely group to be able to continue working from the safety of their homes. As well as suffering record numbers of job losses, along with the economic devastation that went with it, they were also disproportionately found among the essential workers, continuing to go to their workplaces, risking their health and that of their families, in order to survive. With such research in mind, the traditional definition of working class as white men carrying out manual labor no longer made sense to me. In fact, working class today might look far more like a Black, single mother working multiple frontline jobs. Or, it might look like Belly Mujinga, a Congolese journalist—Radio Télévision Nationale Congolaise's first women's sports reporter—turned transport worker upon moving to the United Kingdom. Mujinga died from Covid at just forty-seven because she worked the sort of public-facing hands-on job during a global pandemic that meant she was never guaranteed the safety that is wrapped around an office worker like a blanket. Working class today might even look like Breonna Taylor, roused from her sleep and shot dead in her own apartment for living in a neighborhood where you are always guilty before you are innocent.

Engaging actively with translating texts is a way of directly considering class. Translation allows for a wider readership. And yet, coming back to the idea of a double-edged sword, it can also take a work further away from its true intention and meaning, as was the case with Victoire's recipes being translated against her will. Black women writers in the twentieth century knew this, and so chose to take power into their own hands and translate their works themselves. They ensured that they spoke in their own language, writing their stories in their own words and making them as accessible as possible. In doing this, they shattered the assumption that anyone else, of any class or color, could be relied upon to lift Black women out of their oppression. Instead, as they already knew, given the opportunity—or even just the space—Black women will lift themselves. These foremothers knew that they bore a responsibility to their daughters and their daughters' daughters, an obligation to urge them to carry out their own translation and to remind them that no one would do it for them.

This has reverberated into the twenty-first century, and today, we too bear a responsibility to translate what we are presented with. On September 24, 2020, Louisville police officer Brett Hankison was charged with three counts of "wanton endangerment." The translation—the reality—is that not one of those charges was for the killing of Breonna Taylor.

Hankison was charged for firing into a neighboring apartment. He was charged for the damage to a property but not the damage to a person. Basketball player LeBron James, interviewed on the day of the announcement, said simply that "the walls of the neighbor's apartment are more important than her life . . . justice was met for her neighbor's walls and not her beautiful life."[5] He apologized to Black women in that interview, quoting Malcolm X that the most disrespected woman in America is the Black woman. Finally, in August 2022, charges were brought against all three officers involved in Taylor's killing, but the reality remains that whilst Taylor's family was paid a twelve-million-dollar settlement, it took over two years for them to receive justice. On August 24, 2020, Tamika Palmer, Breonna Taylor's mother, spoke to *Vanity Fair*.[6] She spoke in her own words about her baby. Her baby who didn't cry. Her baby who sang the blues with her own mother's mother, making everyone laugh until they cried with Johnnie Taylor's "Last Two Dollars." The baby she taught to ride a motorcycle. The baby who was bossy and self-assured, determined and driven. *Her* baby who was taken from her—forever—by three counts of wanton endangerment, bullets fired in another direction. My heart is numb. The translation is essential.

Today's inheritors of the Nardal sisters' and Condé's work—engaging with the world on their own terms in their own way—are surprising. There are a few familiar names. First up is Michelle Obama. Even before *Becoming* dropped as a book and then as a tour and then as a Netflix show and a

Spotify podcast, the world could not get enough of her. The press tried to drag her down in the early years of Barack Obama's campaign and presidency, but they couldn't. No "angry Black woman" trope would stick. She is fiercely intelligent, compassionate, and relatable. Her husband was president of the United States of America and yet she has her own firmly distinct legacy. She makes me believe that anything is possible. I can put my words onto paper and I can try to change the world a little bit by working for the United Nations and I can make movies and I can run marathons and I can look good if I feel like it and I can do it all with humor, passion, ferocity, and love. And what is more important than anything I can do—anything that any of us do—is that in weaving this thread of gold we are freeing other Black women to do the same. We are building a tapestry that does not force us to choose. Just like Condé and the Nardals before her, Obama is weaving a narrative that says that we can be both— all—everything. Her whole being, everything she is and does, is about connecting with people. It is about joining the formation, creating the opportunities and space for Black women to lift themselves up.

Yara Shahidi, activist and influencer, does this, too. A quick glance at her Instagram shows you what she is about: Her little squares are a tribute to and celebration of Blackness—a means of inspiring change. Social media activism is a tricky one to get right; the blackout day in the wake of George Floyd's killing proved that. I would see people I knew full well had touched my hair or told me that they could never bring a Black partner to meet their parents post their little black square—and that hurt. Solidarity is important, but change won't come as easily as shutting off your Instagram account for a day. Shahidi, however, grabs her account by the reins and harnesses its power, galvanizing her millions of followers into action along the way. Her granddad spent time with the Black Panthers in their heyday and she is fearlessly continuing his legacy. In high school she started Yara's Club, a partnership with the Young Women's Leadership Network, which provides online mentorship with the goal of ending poverty through education. For her birthday in 2018, she launched Eighteen × 18, a national initiative that encourages young people to work together to make a change in their local communities by getting involved in local and national politics. She frequently speaks out against the desperate injustices occurring in Iran. What she is doing—what we should all be doing—is speaking to young Black women and young people in their own language. Just as Jeanne and Paulette Nardal before her, she is translating her publication for the twenty-first-century audience, allowing them to receive her message in a way that they will appreciate and understand. She creatively provides the space—quite literally in her Instagram squares—and hosts her own salon, bringing together people from all walks of life across the world.

This is power. This is Black female power. Just like the Nardal sisters at the start of the previous century, we can actually see Black women not only as literal translators of existing languages, but as translators creating a new language—balancing the intricate difference between class, race, and gender. This is a unique form of translation that bridges the divide of geography, language, and culture. It is revolutionary, uniting Black women not only in their struggle to create their own space, but in securing it for their future, for their daughters. In engaging in both literal and metaphorical border crossing and nationalism, Black women writers, cooks, intellectuals, entrepreneurs, and influencers demonstrate that they will inhabit their rightful space. It is a matter of time. Just as reading *Victoire* that summer while kneading flour and water to make dumplings quite possibly saved me, so can the prolific and pioneering work of Black women in the twentieth century bring renewed hope. They actively and self-consciously engaged in traveling, disrupting the notion of living separate isolated lives to instead show the importance of being connected.

In understanding the global connections between the likes of the Nardals and Victoire, we come closer to understanding the political, literary, and philosophical circles that were exploring what it meant to be a "New Negro" as a Black woman. Obama and Shahidi have inherited their legacies by becoming part of this same movement of Black women who liberate themselves—and by doing so give other Black women permission to do the same. This radical re-creation of the space they inhabit provides a way for Black women to transcend social boundaries and make a better life for those who come next. Aided one hundred years ago by the Black transnational press and a century later by its modern-day descendant, social media, these women engage with race, gender, and class to harness a modernity that is by necessity global and multifaceted. They pave the way for a future of resistance, their united front their strongest asset. In keeping with the choreography of the perfect formation, we return almost full circle, to the words of Beyoncé herself: "Always stay gracious, best revenge is your paper."[7]

Chapter Five

WARRIOR

I WAS IN THE HAIRDRESSER'S recently, sitting back and soaking in the chatter and the languages and the movement—the buzz—of the space where Black women pass in and out, leaving a trail of energy in their wake. There is a purpose to their movements and I have always been fascinated by this as a space. Women arriving one way and leaving another. It is a space where I like to sit quietly, sometimes with a book but often just with myself and my thoughts. Hands in lap, I listen. I observe. My hairdresser is Ghanaian and her salon is a real melting pot of languages and dialects, where Akan mixes with Dagbane, which fuses with English, and the scent in the air of someone microwaving their rice and jerk chicken. It is a coming together of differences: different people and noises and words. Often these languages pass me by, swirling past. But, increasingly, I can pick out odd words and that feels good. In any case, it is a space where I belong. They welcome me in. I like that.

This particular Saturday I am sitting and I don't feel as good as usual. I am tired. With a busy day ahead, I have correctly gambled that I need to be first in that chair to avoid spending a moment longer than I need to in the salon. So, I arrive first thing in the morning and am sitting in the chair with my copy of Warsan Shire's new book but I am not really reading it. The world is happening around me rather than with me being a part of it—that feeling of watching yourself as though through a pane of glass. And then, amid the usual hubbub and laughter interspersed with the occasional raised voice, the door swings open and a little girl bursts in followed by her mother. Her mum has hardly even said good morning to the room when this tiny little girl peeks out from behind her mum's legs and imperiously declares with the energy of a thousand queens: "My hair is nice!" before hiding behind her mum and silently daring us to defy her. Perhaps unsurprisingly, the entire room of women adore this, applauding and cheering her. "Yeeeeeeees!" They laugh. "Yes, it is!" Satisfied, the little girl feels brave enough to step out from behind her mother's legs and grin, perhaps buoyed by the knowledge that her hair *is* nice and she will not have to sit through any treatment in the hairdresser's. She has spared herself.

I love the simplicity of this encounter: A girl came into a hairdressing salon and already liked the way she looked. Every single woman in that salon chose to celebrate that little girl and her choice to declare that she looked good. She didn't want to change herself in any way and I think they all saw and respected that. Looking deeper, even though we all laughed and cheered in the very particular way that adults do when small children say something that they find amusing, I think there was also something in us that thought, *Wow. Good for you*. Every single woman in the salon that day would spend hours in there at a minimum. Weaves, braids, treatments, relaxers. Each hairstyle takes painstaking minutes. It requires giving over entire days. Props to the five-year-old who decided she didn't want to spend her Saturday trapped in a salon— props to the little girl who single-handedly turned against the tide. More important, though, the response was felt on a profound level. It was a wave of women who recognized her rejection of the structures that bound her.

Sitting in the hairdressing chair, halfway through getting my hair braided and staring at myself in the mirror, it got me thinking. I suppose I can consider myself lucky in the sense that I (mostly) like the way I look. I look in a mirror and feel good. I could attribute this to many things: DNA, privilege, refusal to care too deeply about what others think, sheer luck even. Actually, though, I think I owe this in large part to the army of women around me. Just like that little girl in the hairdresser's, my aunties raised me to feel worthy and deserving of every good thing that came my way; my cousins were prepared to fight with their bare hands anyone who attempted to hurt me, and my sisters would intersperse unconditional love with regular takedowns, just so I didn't get too big for my boots. Deep down, though, they hold me tight and tell me to love myself. I know that. And so, when I go out or go on a date or even just walk into a room, I carry myself with the energy of someone who already knows "my hair is nice" or, more fittingly in my case: *I* am nice. I like myself and I move through the world holding myself accordingly.

Maybe, just maybe, this realization is more than an innate self-confidence and it is even more than a direct tribute to the women who raised me. Maybe it is also armor. Or survival. Girlboss feminism, also known as choice feminism—a movement that places the individual above the collective—would hold this up, heralding it as a particular brand of self-love, of knowing your worth. We are taught to love ourselves, which also translates into spending money to make ourselves look the way we want or cutting people out of our lives who we don't think are worth our time or spending an entire day sitting at the hairdresser's. The self-care industry is worth billions.

If you type "#selfcare" into Instagram you are met with beauty products, before-and-after fitness posts, and quotes about #lovingyourself so that no one else can ever determine (or depreciate) your worth. Yoga features a lot, as do pictures of people drinking champagne in various luxurious holiday destinations. Imagine the surprise of the brands and the influencers and the general capitalist co-option of self-care and self-love if they knew that its roots were in radical feminist and anti-racist revolutionary politics.

In fact, the concept of self-care was created in 1988 by activist, poet, and writer Audre Lorde. Her quote, or a part of it, anyway—"Caring for myself is not self-indulgence, it is self-preservation, and that is an act of political warfare"[1]—has been much circulated on social media in various contexts. I don't doubt that many people have it as a poster on their walls, or that they archly and wittily quote it as they book a massage or order another round of drinks with their girl-friends. And yes, on the surface it seems powerful in this context. When I think of warfare I imagine bombs, tanks, destruction, and death; I don't think of the simple act of car-ing for myself. But then again, maybe we all misread the memo. In fact, in 1988, when crafting this greatly misquoted concept of caring for oneself, Audre Lorde was suffering from the cancer that eventually killed her. She was stepping back from a lifetime of generosity, of giving, of financially support-ing other women at a time when she could barely even sup-port herself. Lorde was taking herself out of a lifetime of, in her own words, "being invisible"—as a woman, then doubly as a Black woman, and then thrice so as a Black, queer woman. Her essay collection *A Burst of Light: and Other Essays* was partly written to explore her struggles with cancer and the racist and sexist structures that tied her, a lesbian, Black woman, down. It is in the context of this, an aggressive cancer destroying her body from the inside out and an aggressive re-gime seeking to destroy her from the outside in, that she wrote the titular essay in the collection: "A Burst of Light: Living with Cancer." It is in this context that Lorde considers self-care to be both revolutionary and political. It was self-preservation for her because as a Black (and especially as a Black and queer) woman living with cancer, she genuinely needed to preserve all of the energy she possibly could in order to quite literally survive. How have her words been so misinterpreted? This thread of gold that she began weaving as she fought for her own survival has been pulled and twisted in so many directions that it has almost lost its color.

If you look closely enough, though, you can retrieve the shape of its thread, see the faint hue of gold. In that essay, Lorde speaks a lot about "overextension" and of finding herself being pulled too far. I think again of the many times people remark on my busy "superwoman life" and then, swallowing hard, of the cautionary tale bestowed upon me by an actor I was once in a play with. I had bounded into a matinee show in London having raced a half marathon in Oxford that morning, sprinted home in time to shower, and then caught the train to London, making it by the skin of my teeth in time to change into my eighteenth-century costume and perform in a play to the unsuspecting matinee audience. Fellow cast member Elaine was sitting next to me in the dressing room as I was getting my hair done and she listened carefully as I told her about my morning before looking me in the eyes and quietly saying, "Be careful." "What do you mean?" I asked. "My sister was like you when she was younger," she said. "Boundless, limitless energy in her twenties and then chronic fatigue in her fifties. Be careful, darling." I still think about that now. It echoes in my mind alongside Jacqueline's "What is it you feel you have to prove?" Audre Lorde, as she wrote about taking care of herself, was dying of cancer. Was that early demise simply because of a life spent fighting racism and challenging oppressive structures? Did "overextending" herself quite literally kill her? It is not the greatest stretch in the world to assume that the two are somewhat connected.

If this is the case, then real self-care—genuine self-love and caring for ourselves—is way more than taking a luxury holiday or buying a glass of champagne, even if those things might be important in some way. It is actually about refusing to let ourselves burn out. It is about not letting the anti-racist fight grind us down and not needing to prove our own right to exist. It is about not waking up every single day determined to prove to the world that we are good enough and competent enough and *deserving enough*. It is about walking into any room with the energy of that little girl in the hair salon and knowing that we are already enough. And, perhaps, hiding behind our mother's legs if we get weary. Sometimes it is about letting the entire hairdressing salon—the community around us—carry us and lift us with their support. Audre Lorde's thread runs indelibly into Diane Abbott's. Black women and girls who have chosen to love themselves in a world that says Black women are unlovable are undertaking a most radical act of resistance.

We need to start taking care of ourselves in the way that

we take care of each other and we need to show up for the Black women on the front lines who are overexerting to give us a smoother passage. Those who walked so we could run. Or, as Auntie Nomie said at the funeral of my complicated, brilliant, deeply loved uncle Delroy, who left us far too soon due to an entire lifetime of "overexerting": "They crawled through thorns so we could walk on open fields." Not even running, just walking without our feet being cut. That's all. It is thanks to a community of ancestors that we are here. We are nowhere without our village.

Self-care, when viewed in this light, this "Burst of Light" from Audre Lorde, is a groundbreakingly radical act. It is in this context, the simple action of prioritizing care for ourselves, in whatever form that may take, that perhaps we might truly consider the rest of the quote:

> I had to examine, in my dreams as well as in my immune-function tests, the devastating effects of overextension. Overextending myself is not stretching myself. I had to accept how difficult it is to monitor the difference. Necessary for me as cutting down on sugar. Crucial. Physically. Psychically. Caring for myself is not self-indulgence, it is self-preservation, and that is an act of political warfare.

Overextension does not just mean stretching yourself, pushing yourself a little further to see what you're capable of. Overextension is when you no longer even know why you are pushing yourself to achieve these things and do more. When those around you "don't know how you do it" then it is time for you to ask that question of yourself. Audre Lorde's words are situated within a very particular context. She was battling cancer while creating work that still forms the basis of our resistance today. Don't let her work be co-opted. Hold on to it—and place dearly at its heart the collective over the individual. We need to look after ourselves and we need to look out for each other. Not by treating our friends to champagne or gift boxes, although there is a place for that, but rather by the simple act of holding each other, lifting each other up, and working to dismantle the systems of oppression that exhaust, demoralize, and overextend us. We need to collectively create the conditions that allow Black people to thrive. Who and what is in place to lift us up when our governments let us down, or when our workplace overlooks us, or when we are fleeing a war-torn country and they stop us at the border because of the color of our skin? Let us protect not just ourselves but each other. Let us remind each other that we don't have to stretch ourselves until we snap. We have nothing to prove and we can step away from the marathon at any time we choose. We are already enough.

Shortly before she died, Audre Lorde changed her name to Gamba Adisa, which translates as Warrior: She Who Makes Her Meaning Clear. Warrior. In the context of girlboss feminism, this word is overused—or misused. But when I think of Audre Lorde, I like how it feels. Lorde was a warrior.

Fierce and uncompromising. Not always right. Volatile. Deeply angry at times. But, true to its purest meaning, more than just fighting; protecting and serving. Lorde was clear about her journey, who she was and what she stood for, even in her final days on earth.

I think most of us probably have the warrior in us, maybe not just in the sense of going out into battle, but of protecting and serving ourselves and each other. Grounding ourselves, planting our feet, and declaring our presence and existence; making our meaning clear. I trace the tapestry and almost seamlessly find myself running my finger along Nina Simone's thread. A singer, songwriter, pianist, and civil rights activist, Simone is known for her supreme talents—a veritable prodigy—and then later in life for her turbulent and some-what tragic end, eventually dying at seventy just days after she was named an honorary doctor by the prestigious Curtis Institute, a music school that Simone believed had refused her a scholarship as a young woman because of her race and class. Regardless of what was happening on a personal level, her body of work emblematizes the warrior: raw, potent, and unafraid. Most powerful is the distinct feeling that her work could only have come from a Black woman.

In "Mississippi Goddam," probably her most powerful protest song, Simone responded furiously and straight from her soul to the bombing of a Baptist church in Alabama that had taken the lives of four little girls. Perhaps feeling the vis-ceral pain of the song, her friend Dick Gregory observed that no Black man would have dared to write it. If that really is the case, I can't help but wonder why. Does it bring us back to this idea of overextension—of Black women going beyond—stretching themselves until they snap?

Later, in her 1966 album *Wild Is the Wind*, Simone seemed to have an answer to this, making her meaning perfectly clear. Her anthemic song "Four Women" takes the listener through two centuries of Black history in the form of four verses and four women, with each woman representing a stereotype placed upon Black women: Aunt Sarah (the Mammy), Saphronia (the Mulatto), Sweet Thing (the Jezebel), and Peaches (the Sapphire)—and somehow seeming to speak to this idea of radical self-love. From Aunt Sarah, a dark-skinned enslaved Black woman; to Saphronia, with her "yellow" skin and long hair; to Sweet Thing, belonging to "anyone who has money to buy"; and finally, Peaches, tough and unashamedly angry. Four women. Four warriors.

In America in 1966, a new conversation surrounding art was getting underway. The Black Arts Movement was an ideological collective where Black artists and intellectuals came together to organize, study, and think about what a new Black art and Black politics movement might be, creating art that galvanized and initiated real political change. Black self-love became a key part of this, with the catchphrase "Black is Beautiful" becoming both a rallying cry and a celebration—an affirmation. However, many felt that it valued men, masculinity, patriarchy, and heterosexuality in such a way that it created stifling conditions for Black women. In response, Black women started talking back and writing literature and poetry to sing out their pain.

Nina Simone's music can be seen as part of this creative resistance and the larger struggle to promote a culture of self-love among Black women. Especially with a song like "Four Women," you really feel the urgency with which Simone is crying out for us to write our own stories and create our own sense of identity and self-worth. Does that make her a warrior? I think so. Her personal mission was, in many ways, rooted in her own traumas, a call for self-love that she herself had never been shown. Her husband, Andrew Stroud, a biracial man, was deeply critical of her looks, inevitably in some ways causing her to turn that same criticism inward on herself. She felt unattractive because she did not match the typical beauty standards and also because her own husband never seemed to find her beautiful. She felt that from every angle she was undesirable. What started as a deeply personal sorrow became a community-led pain as she realized that hers was a shared experience and so many Black women around her felt the same. For me, "Four Women" is the most powerful sort of song, a personal rumination that exploded out of itself and became an anthem for a generation. It is not a personal rage for Black women to feel unattractive. It is a communal sorrow. A communal sorrow that still manifests itself today in the form of a little Black girl stepping into the hairdressing salon and refusing to change herself being a revolutionary act.

It's a strong word, "revolutionary." It suggests a total about-turn from all that has gone before it, the beginning of something that has not yet been seen. Perhaps we should try to create more about-turns. Perhaps we need to actively put ourselves into situations where we can be revolutionary. Perhaps "revolutionary" could even mean taking ourselves out of contexts that will likely never change.

Every summer when dating show *Love Island* starts up again I tune in for the first few episodes and reflect on the communal pain of Black women being the last to be chosen, or left out entirely of the blonde or brunette "my type on paper," no option C. They arrive, they parade, they stand, they wait: bated breath. And somehow, still, hope resides that this time they won't be left. Another summer of humiliation as they stand—indignation. And they wait. Or, we wait. We wait.

The real question, though, is why do we keep on putting ourselves in the firing line? Why don't we just quit and accept that we don't need to occupy every space? Perhaps overextension applies here, too. Of course we can keep stretching ourselves and trying to make ourselves fit into spaces too small too wide too straight too tight too white, but eventually, inevitably, we will snap. And for what? Then what? I don't actually know how we got here. And more to the point, how do we move away from this? That's the question I think we all really need to be asking. A starting place seems to be that in order to begin stripping away the layers that make up this communal sorrow, we need to at least try to understand where they have come from. Books? Films? Teenage heartbreak? The internalized trauma of a historical legacy of enslaved ancestors? The fact that our idea of what is beautiful was not created by us in the first place? That makes sense, but could we not then just create a new beauty standard? How hard can it really be? For Nina Simone, it ultimately comes down to a lack of two things: confidence and power, making the case that "Black women didn't know what the hell they wanted because they were defined by things they didn't control, and until they had the confidence to define themselves, they'd be stuck in the same mess forever."[2]

Well, fine. Challenge accepted. Let us define ourselves in our own voices and on our own terms. That is a goal I am excited to strive for. Step one: How do we begin to define ourselves? I think it has to start with supporting each other. We know that external unconditional support is not a given. What, then, does it do to our confidence if we know that there is a community around us, a blanket that is there for when we (inevitably) get it wrong, or fall, or even just need a little rest? Surely then we might feel slightly braver? Maybe we would bypass the hours in the salon—or maybe we wouldn't—but such a decision would be closer to something *we* have chosen than that of a workplace or a school with requests for "tidy" or "professional" hair. Or to look "groomed," as my first acting agent pointedly called me up to remind me on more than one (ten) occasion(s). I remember the first time

I dared to speak about that to someone else. It became quickly apparent that it wasn't normal, and that I shouldn't have to stand for it. Eventually I became braver—and stronger. I found a new team to represent me. They laughed, shaking their heads in horror when I told them about the "groomed" comment. I realized I had been naïve, or perhaps I just needed my community around me. Perhaps that would have made me braver.

So step one is to support each other. Nothing more than that. Just by being there we can open up a space, allowing ourselves to figure things out.

Next, step two, is the community. Many animals do this instinctively, living in colonies or groups.

What do each of these groups have in common? They live their lives as a community in order to increase their chances of survival. There is safety in numbers. Working together to hunt for food means a greater chance of success. They raise their children together and help to look after each other. It quite literally helps them to stay alive. I am drawn to elephants, in particular fascinated by how they live in tightly bonded female tribes headed by the eldest female: the matriarch. They stick together no matter what and in the unlikely or desperate situation where they must separate, the matriarch will entrust her daughter to lead the other herd. The two separated groups, known as "bond groups," don't stray farther than a mile from each other and keep in touch at all times. And when the time is right, by pure memory and trust in their unbreakable bond, they will find their way back to each other. In the most extreme and desperate situations, including death, elephants grieve their loved ones just as we do, returning to the spots where they last saw their friend or family member year after year.

So they say that an elephant never forgets but actually this is not far from the truth. Their memory leaves an indelible imprint on themselves and those in their tribes. For me, there is a lot we can take from how elephants live. We can trust in our basic human need to be part of a protective herd, to remain connected.

So far, so good. Where do we go from the establishment of our herd, then? We need to create our own structures. We form our community; we look out for them and they in turn look out for us. And we create our own parameters of a world in which we feel safe, where we can question the things that make us feel uneasy, uncomfortable, unworthy.

I think back now to the boyfriend who very nearly broke me. I know he did things to me that I have never let myself deal with, have never been able to deal with. He liked me because I was small and fragile and he did all he could to keep me that way. He didn't want me if I dared to grow. In fact, he did all he could to make sure that my growth would be permanently stunted.

The mind is a funny thing. I think we are resilient—or resilience manifests itself—in many ways. Denial is powerful, and my mind in particular manages to shut out the thoughts

I don't want to consider—an excellent short-term anti-anxiety medication. Short term. And yet. What next? There are certain things I know to be true. Some years ago I dated someone who was violent toward me. I do know that that is a fact. I also know that in the years since then, I have let myself think about this only twice. The first time, I had met up with three friends, and for some reason, this person had come into my head. On the train back home I took a deep breath, unsure if the number I had would even still be correct, and rang him. He answered, clearly not having my number saved. "Hello. It's Cat," I said. And, perhaps telling me all I needed to know about the answers I was tentatively seeking, he hung up.

The second time was more recent and has been more profound. I have two sisters and we are best friends. We look alike, sound alike, and have an intensely knit bond. Decades of secrets, shared history, and DNA interwoven like a luscious thick braid. Three strands. Recently, for the first time in years, we fell out. It was a strange feeling, so strange in fact that I struggled to even take it seriously as a fact. I couldn't compute that there could be a world in which my sisters and I weren't speaking. Eventually, all keen to put it to bed, we met up for crisis talks. Things did not go to plan. Laura, my middle sister, is endlessly patient, the sort of person who everyone comes to for advice. She always listens. Hannah, the youngest, has a sense of fairness and justice like nobody I have ever met. She speaks her mind. I attempted to explain my feelings to them both—that I felt isolated, unheard, and underappreciated—but I only made things worse and we ended up in a more desperate misunderstanding than we'd been in when I had arrived. Somewhere in the depths of the argument, and feeling that my sisters were forming a tightly walled unit that I was not allowed entry to, I told Laura, through tears, that she was reminding me of the boyfriend I had worked tirelessly to forget. Perhaps I was trying to hurt her. If so, it worked. She took great offense, knowing some of the story that I had blocked from my mind for almost a decade. Hannah, perhaps knowing less, looked at me dismissively and said: "Oh, is that the one who beat you up?"

Time did this really strange thing where it sped up and then slowed down. I saw and felt where I was in minute and intimate detail: the hot, thick, too-early heat wave; the men in front of us, wondering what we were arguing about on a balmy summer evening; the water I couldn't bring myself to sip; the dark, sticky oak of the table. *The one who beat me up?* My mind could not process this. There were a number of levels to it: first that my own sister could speak those words to me, but then also the words themselves—"beat me up"? What was this? Was it true? It couldn't be, could it?

I left, stumbling out in a thick fog of tears that stung me for reasons I could not fully understand. All night I moved between tentatively trying to let my mind go where I had never allowed it to, like when you lost a tooth as a child and your tongue probed the new jellylike piece of flesh, soft where before it had been solid. Fleeting, hazy memories came. A group of two or three girls dragging me to the toilets on a night out, asking me about dating this person and wanting to know if I was "all right." Concern. And some sort of love from them. I felt that. They asked to meet me the next day, all of us agreeing that three A.M. in a nightclub was not the time for such a conversation and they told me that I wasn't the only one. That he had done this to other girls, too.

Still naïve, still disbelieving, I went back to his place and told him about the conversation I had just had. "They're just *feminists*," he said, with as much disgust as one might reserve for terrorists or rapists or any of the -ists that society generally agrees to be b-a-d. *I'm a feminist*, I told myself. *So what do you think of me then?* But of course I didn't say this, because I was cushioning myself in a protective pillow and to say anything at all would be to acknowledge that my pillow wasn't bullet-proof. I was too busy having a nice time and being a strong independent feminist to question the root of all that was hurting me.

The morning after my fight with my sisters I sent a voice note to my best friend Asha. I met Asha during Freshman Week and we became soulmate friends immediately. I'm sure being two of the only Black faces in the elite world of our university had something to do with it. But also, we had the same energy. We made each other cry with laughter. We ate Nutella out of the jar and shared clothes, beds, and secrets. We compared baby pictures and realized that we looked like twins. We sent the pictures to our parents and even they agreed that we looked remarkably alike. In our second year, Asha's dad was diagnosed with sudden and incurable cancer and her mum called me, asking me to take care of her, to look out for my friend. We truly held each other through the highest and lowest of times. So when I realized that I needed to seek answers, I knew that I could ask Asha. Bracing myself for something I might not want to hear, I sent her that voice note, stumbling over every single word and eventually managing to ask if she remembered anything about these events.

Her response really and truly surprised me.

She said that I never properly told her about what happened at the time and that we only ever really spoke about it at a later date. She told me that I would show her bruises but then never want to discuss where they had come from, brushing them off as nothing, refusing to allow her to probe any deeper. I was more shocked still when she pointed out that my opening up to her even in this small way was groundbreaking, that she would like me to be more open. She asked me if I had noticed what a private person I was when it concerned anything difficult I was going through. She shared that she never really knew how I was doing, that there were so many things that she would have liked to talk to me about but that I was just never willing to go there.

I had nothing to say. And so, I went back to my silence. Contemplating and reflecting until eventually I knew that enough was enough. I had to shatter the silence. I had to speak to save myself. And as I hesitantly started to talk, I realized that—however gradual the process might be—I was going to heal. I was surrounded by the protective blanket of my community, of my sisters and of friends like Asha, who I had met when I barely knew who I was. People who had watched over the years as I faced abuse that I could not articulate, championed me as I thrived, and were still standing there. They had my back. I was safe. If you are reading this and relate on any level, please know that you too are safe. The blanket is around you. It might be in an unexpected place, or it might be in the place that you always expected to find it and never cared to look, but it is there. You are safe. Your herd of elephants means that no lion can enter. And if that lion even tries; well, you are surrounded by *feminists*, after all.

My mum's voice comes back to my mind, quoting from her well-worn Bible to declare that "no weapon that is formed against you shall prosper." Isaiah 54:17, in case you were wondering. It is true, though, and we should hold on to these words, hold on to them like a life raft in wild seas, for no weapon that is formed against us shall *ever* prosper.

So step three: We need to tear down the walls that imprison us. Even if it means facing up to uncomfortable truths, or defeating some enemies that we have given space to, allowed to flourish in the sanctuary of our own minds. No longer. Which links rather nicely to the fourth and final step: It is time to build a new narrative.

Where and how do we begin to build? And more important, how do we ensure that we are building not just our own house, but putting bricks aside for those around us? How do we ensure that the individual affirmation of our rebuilding (our hashtag selfcare) becomes a rousing and communal call to arms? I come back to each step that has gone before. We have to support each other. We have to create our own structures and tear down the walls that imprison us. It is time to write our own stories.

In 1968, at the same time that the Black Arts Movement was unfurling and the cries of "Black is Beautiful" were gathering momentum, Audre Lorde was working as a writer in residence at Tougaloo College in Mississippi. During this year she became a part of the response to the movement, reaffirming her commitment to working as a poet and using her writing to challenge the confines of the world around her. More than just writing, though, she was leading workshops with young and politically motivated Black undergraduate students. It was always about more than just herself; Lorde took great responsibility in her role of spreading the message. She was on a mission and she wouldn't be dissuaded.

I also think there is a lot we can learn from Nina Simone's four women themselves: Aunt Sarah, Saphronia, Sweet Thing, and Peaches. Aunt Sarah speaks against the Mammy stereotype, showing us what self-love looked like for Black women at a time when they were enslaved, existing as the property of others. Her back was strong: "strong enough to take the pain," making me think of the backbreaking physical labor and the beatings that these women lived through.

Despite this, Aunt Sarah stands strong as a symbol of Black cultural legacy, her unrepentant and defiant acceptance of her Blackness: "My skin is Black," with all its associated meanings; "my hair is woolly," speaking directly to the very discourse surrounding beauty standards and politics that we are still trying to dismantle an entire century later. Aunt Sarah is every Black woman who looked those beauty standards in the eyes and said, "Nah. Not today." She is Caster Semenya, Serena Williams, Viola Davis; she is strong, deeply talented, and resilient, even though she shouldn't have to be.

Saphronia, a biracial woman, is an embodiment of the tragic mulatto stereotype and speaks to the complexity of being forced to live "between two worlds." The haunting impact of her revelation that her "rich and white" father "forced [her] mother late one night" paints a vivid picture of a fully realized woman who carries generational trauma on her shoulders like a weight—and may have to make complicated choices because of this. She faces the dual complexity of being a Black woman and also knowing that her very existence was born out of darkness. Sociologist, historian, and civil rights activist W. E. B. Du Bois created a concept called double consciousness, and this is a useful frame of reference here. In talking about double consciousness, Du Bois refers to what he calls his "twoness—an American, a Negro; two warring souls,"[3] something that certainly applies to Saphronia's story. However, Nina Simone draws my attention to what Du Bois overlooks: her status as a woman. Simone describes the way in which she herself would look in the mirror and see "two faces, knowing that on the one hand [she] loved being Black and being a woman, and that on the other it was [her] colour and sex which had fucked [her] up in the first place."[4] If we are talking about layers of consciousness, we move from double to triple—and beyond. How does one live with the weight of having different elements of your identity at war with each other? For Saphronia it is her race at war with her class, which is in turn at war with her gender, made even more complicated by her parentage, but the reality is that it is often even more complicated than this; an unstable lived experience, shaped and characterized by varying degrees of oppression.

Sweet Thing, the Jezebel, also has deep, complex layers. She was the most controversial character in the song at the time of its release, causing it to be banned from some radio stations that did not want to play a song so brazenly about sex work. She represents the sad reality where Black women performers were often forced to dance or sing and thus denied the acclaim they deserved for their talent as musicians. In her book on all-women jazz swing bands, *Swing Shift*, writer Sherrie Tucker discusses "the widely accepted version of the jazz-woman as a girl singer, who stands in front of the band rather than among its ranks."[5] Singing was seen as requiring less skill—and being inextricably tied up with sex. This says a lot about the objectification of the Black female body.

Coming back to our warrior Nina Simone, she describes in her autobiography how despite her years of classical training and her desire to be a concert pianist, she was told in no uncertain terms at one of her very first gigs that she would have to sing, something that she took as an insult to her accomplishments as a pianist. With this in mind, Nina Simone's writing of Saphronia and Sweet Thing is her fighting back. The warrior assumes position. Her years of classical training and dedication destroy the long-standing myth that Black people are inherently inclined to entertain; however, her dedication and prodigious talent as a pianist also puts an end to the idea that real musical talent lies solely with the men of the era. At a time when being a talented musician as a woman was associated with sex work and what was seen as a working-class vice, Nina Simone's very existence makes a whole new meaning very clear indeed. She challenges Du Bois's double consciousness, calling instead for a consideration of the added oppression that being a Black woman entails.

Peaches, the last of the four women, and the stereotype of the Sapphire—or the "angry Black woman"—changes the tone for good. Simone's raspy growl as she describes how she is angry immediately suggests something has shifted. What I see in Peaches's anger is really her rejection of the notion that Black women should feel shame or pain. Instead she turns this pain into a reclamation of Black female personhood, blazing anger intact, and uses it to rewrite her story. As Peaches screams, I hear a woman who will take no more. In her final tribute to the listener, a cacophonous, discordant scream saturated with the oppression of her ancestors that "my name is

PEACHES!," Simone achieves the ultimate reclamation; she invokes the revolution. A rallying cry, the rhythm of her rage becomes communal as Peaches epitomizes the possibility, agency, and power of these four women. Rather than depicting the stereotypes of four static images of Black womanhood, "Four Women" gives us four living, fire-breathing women who have been dealt life's worst hand and yet continue fighting, demonstrating resilience at every step of the way.

What Nina Simone leaves us with is the feeling that the power is in our grasp. We have everything we need within us to (re)claim our own beauty—and to fight for our joy. We don't have to be talked out of ourselves. We are already enough. Buoyed by the glowing feeling that this gave me, I spoke to fifty Black women from across the world, connected via social media, my hairdresser, my running club, my workplaces, my friends, and everywhere in between. I asked them three simple questions:

- What does beauty mean to you?
- What do you find beautiful about yourself?
- What do you do to embrace your beauty?

The results were humbling. I learned that for so many of the women I spoke to, beauty is a feeling—and one that can be found in everyone. There is a generosity to beauty that many of the women I interviewed wanted to hold on to. The following are just a few snippets of the conversations I had.

What does beauty mean to you?

- I think beauty is a feeling. It can be found everywhere and it can be found in everyone.

- For me, I just never really grew up feeling like I fit into traditional beauty standards. Maybe that came from growing up and being one of the only brown kids. Some of it is how I am as a person. I've always been seen as one of the boys and quite nurturing and traditional. I've never really fit into what I saw beautiful people look like. But growing up, it has meant that I have put less of a thing on it: Beauty is a feeling, it's when you are somewhere amazing, or you try on something different.

- Beauty to me can be physical or it can be a moment that makes me feel warm inside. The thing that comes to my mind is when you are around friends and you just feel warmth: It feels like you can take a step outside of yourself and see it as though it is a picture and it just feels like something that you want to remember.

- I'm a sucker for things that are aesthetically nice. That could be something in nature or it could be a really nice house that has the right vibe and energy.

- Beauty to me is about confidence, self-love, but also about loving others and having a good heart. You're not beautiful in my eyes if your heart is ugly.

- With people, beauty for me is formed from characteristics—people who give you that warm, fuzzy feeling.
- For me, beauty is from within. Things are changing and have for the last twenty years but I really never saw myself in what was typically beautiful. I always saw beauty as blond hair, blue eyes, white skin— everything that I'm not. But as I got older I started learning that beauty was from within. I think over the last five to six years I have learned that the things that make people beautiful are being kind, generous, caring.

What do you find beautiful about yourself?

- I find "what do you find beautiful about yourself?" a really hard question. I think the thing I would connect most to aesthetically is my hair. And that's because of the link to our ancestors. Like I don't think I could ever shave my head, I feel quite emotionally invested in my hair. I find that a really hard question. It's harder than considering what I like about myself.
- I think I'm quite a thoughtful person. I crave connection and meaning and I think that is really beautiful.
- I am an extremely caring person. I wear my heart on my sleeve.

- Physically I love my body and my skin. It's taken me a long time to accept my skin color but I think it's deep and beautiful. Emotionally I think I have nice energy. I feel like I'm warm and accepting.
- I think my energy is beautiful. I am filled with a zest for life and I want to grab it for as long as I possibly can. People always say my happiness is infectious.
- I think I'm a great listener, which is kind of beautiful. Not everyone can say that.

What do you do to embrace your beauty?

- To embrace my beauty I like to try things, I like to wear really bright colors and do different things. I like to experiment with things that are maybe nontraditional.
- I think I feel most beautiful when I feel good in myself, so I try to always do things that make me feel good.
- I am lucky that I was raised by a mother who loved me and was proud of me and always talked about my good qualities. I think she taught me to love myself—and just that act of loving yourself is a way to embrace your beauty.
- I take care of myself in terms of the physical—hair, nails, exercise—but really I stay in touch with my emotions.

- I go to therapy!
- To embrace my beauty I like to look after myself. I like fashion, I do my skincare and makeup. The process of doing my skincare and makeup especially makes me feel beautiful and relaxed—it's like a reminder to my brain that I'm taking care of myself.

I think what came out more than anything else from the beautiful conversations I had about the beautiful ways these beautiful women embraced their beauty is that being able to embrace beauty is something that we actively have to work at. In Yoruba culture they say, "Asè." It means the power to make things happen through your actions and intentions.

I like that. I like the optimism of it. Just like the four women who came before, the fifty women who come after, and the generations still to come, we have the power within us, both to invoke a revolution or to quietly, gradually heal. Change is whatever we need it to be, and most important of all: It is already within us. It is ours to mold, shape, and craft. Just like that little girl in the hairdressing salon, we are enough, just as we are. Warriors, come forth.

Chapter Six

QUEEN

I N DECEMBER 2020, WHEN many of us were locked deep in the confines of our homes and the inescapable torture of our minds, a Netflix show burst onto our TV screens and took the world by storm. *Bridgerton*, for more reasons than one, was the talk of the town. It was racy and sexy, depicting sex in the constraints of a period-drama world at a time when sex in real life with anyone we didn't live with was banned and the nation was, quite frankly, bored. It also piloted something called color-conscious casting, where central characters were racially diverse with little to no need for justification; they just were. This didn't always work, namely because it was commented on intermittently in a way that made for confusing stakes; either race mattered or it didn't.

Either way, a cultural conversation was started. Particularly interesting in all of this was the depiction of Queen

Charlotte of Mecklenburg-Strelitz as biracial in the show, which went beyond color-conscious casting, for Charlotte is widely believed to be Britain's first biracial queen. Behind the scenes of the Netflix drama, the life of the real Queen Charlotte was an interesting one: She directly opposed slavery, informally worked as a botanist, had fifteen children, loved music—and may well have had African ancestors. She was also an immigrant, arriving in England from Germany and becoming queen at just seventeen years of age. Despite her accomplishments, the physical descriptions of her from the time are insulting. She has been described as anything from "plain and undesirable" to "small and crooked, with a true mulatto face," "ill colored" and with a nose that was "too wide" and lips that were "too thick."[1] Beyond their derogatory undertones, the racial connotations of these descriptions no doubt contribute to the belief that Charlotte might have been Black, but what other evidence is there for this? Where did this line of thinking come from? One historian in particular, Mario de Valdes y Cocom, is widely credited with bringing this theory to life. He suggests that Charlotte's features were unmistakably Black, also pointing to the descriptions of her contemporaries. His theory, which is increasingly held to be founded in truth, is that she is a direct descendant of the Portuguese royal family, who had African origins.

The possibility of Charlotte being Black becomes more interesting in the wake of Meghan Markle, a biracial American woman who joined—and fairly rapidly left—the British royal family and subsequently spoke out about the reality of becoming part of such an institution as someone who was not white. I still far too frequently hear Brits, decked out in their England kit and flying high the flag of St. George, state that "obviously" they are not racist but "you know, we're a white country. Just look at our royal family." I often take a delicious satisfaction in pointing out that the British royal family is actually German. That soon puts an end to any wartime nationalist fantasies. Still, though, what an odd realization that the country of my birth prefers not to believe that their royal family could ever look anything like me.

More to the point, they fail to even consider that Black and brown people might have an institution such as a monarchy of their own. In England, at least, it is seen as something intrinsically British—a monarch who rules far beyond the waves of their native small island, universally revered. A Dave lyric comes to mind: "Tell us we used to be barbaric, we had actual queens."[2] I think of my own mum, nicknamed from birth Queenie for her beauty. We have a rich and proud history of queens who look like us. Dating back hundreds and even thousands of years, the imprint left by these fearless women is there for anyone who cares to look deep enough. These visionary leaders are a source of strength and a fierce means of rebuttal for any narrative that centers enslavement and oppression over empowerment. We can take a little time to hold up the lineage of women such as Queen Ana Nzinga of Ndongo (now Angola), or Queen Nzinga as she was known in her country. She was a fearless politician, military leader, and diplomat, and was a key player in Angola's resistance of Portuguese influence. Thanks to her, many of her people were spared enslavement. She was eloquent and charming and because of this was able to pull together a long list of allies whom she would continue to draw on as she worked toward the liberation of her country.

Yaa Asantewaa, also known as the queen mother of Ejisu in the Ashanti empire, was another fearless leader, holding the second-highest position in the entire empire. In 1900, she led the Ashanti war against British colonials. Queen Yaa Asantewaa was responsible for presiding over what is known as the Golden Stool, the throne of the Ashanti people, which established power, culture, and stability within the land. She was a leader who was known to challenge, questioning outdated gender roles and advocating for more women in power.

Then there are women who are not technically royalty in the traditional sense of the word but whose legacy brings us close to an alternative understanding of it: those who have received the highest of accolades and should rightfully be lauded for them. Political activist Wangari Maathai, an ecofeminist who combined environmental protection with human rights, is one such individual. Born in Nyeri, Kenya, in 1940, Maathai holds the honor of being the first woman in East and Central Africa to have gained a doctorate degree and the first African woman to receive the Nobel Peace Prize. She started her life raised by nuns in a Kenyan village before winning a scholarship to study in the United States. After spending years teaching veterinary anatomy she eventually became chair of her department and an associate professor in 1976 and 1977, respectively. In both cases, she was the first woman to achieve those positions in that region. It wasn't smooth sailing, though. A job offer at the University of Nairobi was withdrawn as Maathai was seen as having too much ambition for a woman. She found a job in a different department before realizing that she was paid less than her male colleagues as well as being denied pension payments and medical insurance for her family. Seeking a way of fighting back against this, and also understanding that other women in Kenya felt that they did not have enough food to eat or options to take their situation into their own hands, Maathai responded by launching a campaign to prevent deforestation. Working from the belief that "poor people will cut the last tree to cook the last meal. . . . The more you degrade the environment, the more you dig deeper into poverty,"[3] she mobilized Kenyan women to take personal action by planting trees and, in the process, providing themselves with a means of making a living. Over nine hundred thousand Kenyan women have benefited from being able to sell seedlings, and the initiative, dubbed the Green Belt Movement, has made its way across the entire African continent, resulting in the planting of more than thirty million trees, and, spearheaded by the United Nations, over eleven billion trees worldwide. It wasn't just about planting trees, though. It was about a global empowerment of women and a shifting of perspective whereby African women could come together and become agents of change not just for themselves but for the generations to come. Tree planting became a symbol of women's rights, it became a movement of solidarity, and it became a way of leaving an imprint—or weaving a tapestry. Maathai's very last wish, even as she lay on her deathbed in the final stages of cancer, was that she would not be buried in a wooden coffin. She held true to the convictions of a lifetime, even in the face of death. I am drawn to the words of Nigerian environmental activist Nnimmo Bassey, who remarked: "If no one applauds this great woman of Africa, the trees will clap." Well, if the trees are applauding, I am doing so with them. I am on my feet for Maathai, a standing ovation for her honor. Stand with me. Applaud Maathai's legacy, polish its shine as we pull forth her thread into the urgent climate journey that lies ahead of us.

Maybe this is the real role of a queen: More than an accident of birth, perhaps a queen should lead her people with integrity, advocate for substantial change, be able to withstand criticism, and bring people together in the process.

Florynce "Flo" Kennedy, lawyer, activist, civil rights advocate, lecturer, and feminist, knew something about this. Never seen without her cowboy hat, Kennedy was a proud eccentric who embodied genuine inclusion. In 1944 Kennedy began classes at Columbia, majoring in prelaw and graduating in 1949. However, when she applied to the university's law school, she was refused admission. She complained, unequivocally stating that she felt she had been rejected because she was Black, to which the associate dean, Willis Reese, told her that she had been rejected "not because [she] was a Black but because [she] was a woman."[4] Kennedy's response was to write him a letter saying that whatever the reason was, it felt the same to her. Refusing to take no for an answer, she threatened to sue the university and was offered a place on the spot: the only Black woman in her class. Writing about it later, she aptly said: "I find that the higher you aim, the better you shoot."[5]

After graduating in 1951, Kennedy opened her own office, working on criminal cases but also challenging the media and empowering individuals to share information and protest racism in advertising. Clients she represented ranged from the Black Panthers to Billie Holiday and Charlie Parker. She even filed a lawsuit against the Roman Catholic Church for threatening women's reproductive rights.

Kennedy channeled an intersectional approach to activism. She refused to simply go along with the predominantly white feminist movement of the time and instead brought the lessons of Black Power to white feminism, building bridges in the struggles against racism and sexism as she went. Describing her own mission, she said: "My main message is that we have a pathologically, institutionally racist, sexist, classist society. And that n——izing techniques that are used don't only damage Black people, but they also damage women, gay people, ex–prison inmates, prostitutes, children, old people, handicapped people, Native Americans. And that if we can begin to analyze the pathology of oppression . . . we would learn a lot about how to deal with it."[6]

Her methods were defiant and daring. She was an outspoken activist who summed up her protest strategy as "making white people nervous" and even infamously staged a mass urination—or "the Great Harvard Pee-In"—to protest the lack of female bathrooms at Harvard University. When she traveled the lecture circuit in the seventies with Gloria Steinem and was asked (by men) if the pair were lesbians, Kennedy's delicious answer was the simple question: "Are you my alternative?" Whilst employing her acerbic wit, Kennedy also managed to unite across boundaries, bringing white feminists, Black men, and gay rights advocates together to join the Black feminist movement. She used her larger-than-life personality to bring attention to the causes that she was fighting for. In 1974, *People* magazine referred to her as "the biggest, loudest and, indisputably, the rudest mouth on the battleground where feminist activists and radical politics join in mostly common cause."[7] Kennedy was, of course, thrilled with the description. Just like Hattie McDaniel, Kennedy knew who she was and she never apologized for it, saying of herself: "I'm just a loud-mouthed middle-aged colored lady with a fused spine and three feet of intestines missing, and a lot of people think I'm crazy. Maybe you do too, but I never stopped to wonder why I'm not like other people. The mystery to me is why more people aren't like me."[8]

Kennedy used her voice prolifically and fearlessly. She was loud and unashamed. She found her power in making her presence felt. I enjoy her bravery, her trust in her own voice, and her disregard for what anyone might think of her. It sings out to me as unabashed, unashamed joy. I also acknowledge that this is not the only way. For every forthright Kennedy, there are the quiet women: loners, thinkers, and introverts. Like Michaela Coel, there are examples of women who found their power in buckling down, keeping to themselves, and seeing what came from the silence. Black women video gamers are one such group who are often overlooked, but they too have left their trail of gold in the tapestry.

In the 1980s, French-Caribbean Muriel Tramis made history as the first Black woman video-game designer. After studying engineering at the Higher Institute of Electronics in Paris and working for five years at an aerospace company, she developed her first video game, *Méwilo*, followed by the adventure strategy game *Freedom*. Both games were inspired by her home country of Martinique, introducing countless gamers to the island for the first time and inspiring a generation of Black women gamers who came after her. Twenty years later, Amira Virgil, also known as XMiramira, was inspired by Tramis's legacy and developed skin tone modifications for Black and brown players of *The Sims*, having noticed how hard it was to create characters with a specific skin tone. Her response was to create the Melanin Pack, which allowed for the development of darker skin tones and was eventually adopted in August 2020 by Electronic Arts, home of Maxis, the developer of *The Sims*.

The image of these loner Black women, in their dark rooms quietly coding and building what will become entire worlds, is a fascinating one. When you think about it, they're not all that different from the very visible queens who went before them. From racially diverse period-drama characters, to the inference that Britain might have had a biracial queen, to the powerful leaders defending entire countries and the loudest and quietest of us weaving the tapestry, being respected as a queen or as a leader, they are each united by a world of possibility.

Possibility to me speaks of nuance. Often it is far, far too easy to dismiss oppression in terms of definitions of inequality that have little bearing on day-to-day lived experience. Black people are oppressed because society is racist. Women are oppressed because society is sexist. Queer people are oppressed because society is homophobic and trans people because society is transphobic. All of these statements are true, and yet what this does in practice is fail to acknowledge what the reality or the feeling of these words is. I have heard countless intellectual debates about whether the royal family is racist, but might we rather talk, for example, on a human level about the family you marry into wondering what color skin your child might have? Or, the possibility that your heritage might be airbrushed from history to better fit the ideals of what a royal should look like? What does that actually feel like—and how does articulating this help us move forward?

Gladys Bentley, a blues singer and entertainer born in 1907, is someone who articulated such feelings and made a difficult decision to acknowledge what she was willing to withstand, walking away from that which surpassed her limits. Dubbed "Harlem's most famous lesbian"[9] by *The New York Times*, Bentley was one of the most financially successful Black women in the United States in the 1920s and '30s. She was also the first prominent performer of her era to truly embrace a gender-fluid identity. Despite her fame at the time, she is nowhere near as well known today as some of her Harlem Renaissance contemporaries, such as Bessie Smith and Zora Neale Hurston. Her legacy has faded into relative obscurity. This could be attributed to her risqué performances, where she would often gender bend traditional blues numbers and sing lewd versions of popular songs—to the delight of her audience—or it could be attributed to the fact that at a certain point, Bentley "quit" the life she had built for herself. Bentley walked away from her own identity. An openly gay woman who proudly loved other women, wore men's clothing, and in many ways made a name for herself because of, not in spite of, this, Bentley would surprise audiences with her attire, her deep growling voice, and her extraordinary talent as a pianist and singer. Harlem socialite Harold Jackman wrote of her: "When Gladys sings 'St. James Infirmary' it makes you weep your heart out."[10]

Dressed head to toe in immaculate white dress shirts with stiff collars and Eton jackets, Bentley would tantalize her audiences by flirting with women and telling them that she had married a white woman, her refusal to care what anyone thought only adding to her intrigue. But, as the roaring twenties came to a close and the misery of the Great Depression set in, something shifted. Tolerance waned. Bentley was no longer allowed to perform wearing men's clothing unless she carried a special permit. She was frequently abused when she did perform. Eventually, in a 1952 *Ebony* magazine article entitled "I'm a Woman Again," she described the torture of struggling with her gender identity, disclosing that she had taken female hormones and had "cured" herself,[11] posing in a dress with flowers in her hair as though to drive her point home. She claimed to have had male partners and even married twice (although both men denied this) and, before her untimely death from flu at the age of fifty-two, was studying to become a church minister.

Try as I might, I cannot get my head around this transformation. Why did she have to renounce her existence? What did such a statement do to those who might have been looking up to her as proof that their own existence mattered? I can't help but feel bitterly disappointed. Why couldn't Bentley have stuck it out? Then I catch myself mid-thought. We are quick to dismiss people who "quit" and I am not really sure why. This is a woman who had spent decades pioneering what gender could look like if removed from its traditional binary. She was one of the most successful performers of the Harlem Renaissance and to this day is an unsung hero of the LGBTQIA+ community. At a time when it was becoming increasingly difficult for Bentley to continue existing, perhaps she quite simply opted for self-preservation. Perhaps, in walking away from the life she had forged, she was making an active choice to protect herself.

We all stand to learn from listening to each other. From hearing comes understanding. I think of a trip abroad with friends a couple of years back. We were exhausted, but it was that jarring mixture of being tired from the previous night out while knowing that it was our last night and so not wanting to give in to the obviously sensible solution, which would have been to go to bed. Instead, we sat around talking about everything in the frank, unfiltered way that comes from exhaustion and being in a group that you no longer even need to try around. The conversation turned to some of the abuses faced by so many women—and we came to realize that so many of us knew what sexual assault looked like in some form or another. Every single person at that table had their own story. What made the discussion more horrific—more traumatic—was the fact that there was a real simplicity to the discussion of how it *felt*. It was one of those conversations that at the time numbs you but later replays on a loop like the worst kind of nightmare. Are women's lives that worthless?

Too many of us have a story. Getting lost in these thoughts took me down a deep hole on my flight home. I started to panic and feel overwhelmed with the darkness of it. There are people in this world who mean to cause us harm. There are people who will not sympathize when bad things happen. These are indisputable facts. But when my loved ones hurt, I hurt. You hurt them and you hurt me. How, then, are we supposed to carry on? How do we navigate each day when we live with the knowledge of what is out there, the knowledge that the world can be cruel? Perhaps we make the difficult choice to simply opt for kindness for ourselves. I imagine a world where Gladys Bentley went home at night, shook off whatever the world had thrown at her that day, and gowned herself again in her white tuxedo, standing tall, standing strong—even if just for herself.

I begin to take solace in the power of being able to speak frankly. Not to theorize in terms of "sexism" or "racism" but to simply describe how something makes me feel—or to step away if a situation is causing me harm. I loop back full circle to my earlier observation: Taking ourselves out of circumstances that will likely never change is a revolutionary act. Maybe we don't have to know why something happens, or even what it is; just articulating how it makes us feel is a start.

I take comfort in seeing examples throughout history of women who have done just this. Like Muriel Tramis, there are women who find their way in quiet and methodical thought processes. There are people whose simple expression forms the basis of their dignified and grounded truth. I remember I used to write letters to myself. I delighted in writing to "future me" because I would find it reassuring for my present self to look back to me in the past and know that no matter what "past me" was going through she had made it to this point. When I was living in Paris I used to take this one step further with my friends Soraya and Katie, filming video diaries for our "future selves," always signing off with "love you, future self." It sounds ridiculous now—we knew it was ridiculous then—but I love looking back on it and seeing this simple act of declaring love: speaking honestly about how we felt and doing so for no one other than ourselves.

I recently had the honor of visiting Ethiopia on my first official UN mission, attending the Third Africa Forum on Women, Peace and Security. From pretty much the moment I got off the plane I realized that this trip was going to be special. From South Africa to Libya to Uganda to Zambia, women were attending from every country on the continent. With the aim of leveraging women's participation in peace processes, both in Africa and across the world, the entire forum was filled with peacekeepers, leaders, ministers—change makers in every sense of the word. Ellen Johnson Sirleaf, former president of Liberia, Nobel Peace Prize laureate, and the first elected female head of state on the entire African continent, opened proceedings. Known for leading Liberia through the Ebola outbreak, Johnson Sirleaf was awarded the Presidential Medal of Freedom, the United States's highest civil award, for her personal courage and unwavering commitment to expanding freedom and improving the lives of people in Liberia and across Africa. In her speech, she challenged us to dream bigger, not to wait to be invited in: "Africa now knows what a woman president can do." To see Johnson Sirleaf alongside the likes of the African Union's special envoy on Women, Peace and Security, Madame Bineta Diop; Sahle-Work Zewde, president of Ethiopia; and Phumzile Mlambo-Ngcuka, former executive director of UN Women, ignited something in me.

As the forum unfolded and we began to exchange on how to ensure that women are meaningfully engaged in bringing about lasting peace, the commitment and renewed energy of these leaders became apparent.

As the youngest person in the room by quite some decades, I sat back in wonder at these matriarchs who had contributed to the very creation of the thread of gold. Sahle-Work Zewde acknowledged the extraordinary legacy left both behind and ahead of her. Speaking to the elders in the room, some in their eighties and still leading the charge for women's rights across Africa, she declared: "We are here because we rose on your shoulders. We see what you did in your country. Let me reassure you that we will continue to stand on your shoulders. And I tell my sisters present here: You can also stand on mine." The president of Ethiopia recognized those who came before and how we will continue to pave the way for those who come after. It is only through the literal process of lifting each other up—and articulating this shared understanding—that we will continue to progress, to move beyond. I was humbled by the women in front of me and approach my own work with renewed zeal. "I retire but I'm not tired" reverberated in my head throughout the forum. These are women who hold tight to their thread and weave it in full, glorious color: eighty years of age with the energy of a twenty-year-old. They are changing the world. We should revere them.

Perhaps what was most remarkable in the context of such a high-level event was the sheer joy that abounded. We would go from discussing the desperate plight of young girls being married off before they had even started their periods to celebrating the United Nations Female Police Officer of the Year to dancing until we cried with laughter to "Jerusalema." We would get in the minibus at the end of each day and howl at the stories that we shared, those that only come out in women-centric spaces. *These women are this thread of gold*, I told myself. And gold is right. They are shining. They are joy. Even among the most prestigious of leaders, in the most formal of circumstances, at the most desperate of times, *we still find our joy*.

Una Marson was a poet, social worker, and activist who at twenty-three became the first female editor-publisher in Jamaica. She made history as the first Black woman to be invited to the League of Nations and went on to work for the League's Information Section for three months in 1935. As Italy prepared to invade Ethiopia, Marson returned to London to volunteer for the Ethiopian ambassador and accompanied

Emperor Haile Selassie back to Geneva as his personal secretary. She too wrote to herself, beautifully, of Black women's agency and the inherent power in speaking. One poem in particular, "Black Burden," speaks of the importance of Black women coming together. Regardless of how loud their voice is, their collective liberation comes from them articulating, sharing, laughing, and freeing themselves. "Black girl—what a burden," Marson cries out, acknowledging the weight that Black women carry. Just that acknowledgment and empathy— that sense of feeling seen—can be the first step to a healing journey, a rooting of the self in a place of calm. Then, as though sensing how her words might soothe her reader, Marson takes it one step further: She holds us up.

She writes, "Black girl, your burden / Will fall from your shoulders," and she goes on to reassure the reader that she has all that she needs, as she has love in her soul and in her heart.[12]

I feel soothed by the thought of a song in my heart, tenderly placed there by a generation of women who came before me, vigorously sung out by the generation who came after, passed down for those still to come. I am transported back to my time in Ethiopia. A song called "Superwoman" by a network of Tanzanian women—and all of us united in our joy at hearing it, dancing to it, believing in its lyrics. I think of my own songs, my own stories. Those I have already written and those I am yet to write. I read them, sing them, write them, leaving my legacy as I do so. Being a queen is more than simply leading your country to victory. Being a queen also means knowing when to speak and when to stay silent. It is built upon contentment in solitude, but also accountability for your actions. It might mean turning your back on all that you thought you wanted—or all that you had previously known. But crucially, it is always born out of a genuine hope that things will get better; that there is a brighter way.

The funny thing is that when I look back now at those letters I used to write to myself, I feel a profound connection between the person I was and the person I have become—and am becoming. Maybe I couldn't see it then, but I now see quite unmistakably that each one of those letters embodies hope. I am drawn to one in particular:

> In fact, maybe the trick in life is to try new things and to go into them with the confidence shining out of you as though you have done them before and will do them again and again and again. You can try anything. The world is open, and it is yours.
>
> On your darkest days and at your lowest points and when nothing else seems to matter, be a light for yourself and you will light the way for others. Everything else will follow.

I could get on board with that. It brings me back again to the idea of possibility. If we can examine the evidence and see the very real possibility of a biracial queen, or a Black woman taking on the climate crisis, or challenging the rigid notion of how gender is performed, or crying with laughter in a minibus after a day putting the world to rights, then we are existing in a space where we, too, possess the possibility of being part of the change. We are part of the movement, whether it comes from shouting at the top of our lungs or silently keeping on keeping on, beyond the realm of what seems possible. Our joy is a presence and our very presence is a light, a reminder that we are here: a delicate, flickering, but still shining thread of gold.

Chapter Seven

PIONEER

W HEN I WENT SWIMMING for the first time it felt like freedom. I can still remember five-year-old me bouncing in my car seat, the sharp tang of chlorine as I entered our local leisure center, and the bright, harsh lights and loud, excited voices. I remember changing in the humid cubicles and taking extra care to walk not run as I made my way to the edge of the pool, even though everything in me wanted to run—to fly, even. Fast-forward ten years or so and the place of my childhood jubilation was a prison for my teenage self. My freshly relaxed hair would be destroyed the moment water so much as touched it. And if I didn't wear it straight then my swimming cap wouldn't fit over my Afro. I couldn't win. There was no one I could ask for advice about this. The other girls had the sleek, straight hair I burned my scalp every six weeks to get. They wouldn't understand. I started hiding in the changing rooms, correctly making the gamble that my swimming teacher wouldn't follow up on my absence if I showed my face every once in a while. Eventually, hating everything about the tight lanes, the tight swimming caps, and the tightness of the space itself, I began to recognize that the brightness—or possibly even the whiteness—of the swimming pool made no space for me. So I stopped. For almost the next decade, this was how things stayed. Swimming was not for me.

Then, in January 2020, as the earliest strains of coronavirus—at that time still nothing more than an unfamiliar word at the bottom of the weekly news cycle—began to enter our consciousness, my complicated, brilliant, deeply loved uncle Delroy died without warning. It was so unexpected that when I found out, all I could manage to mutter was: "What? What? What?" I didn't understand. We had just been together at Christmas, ten days earlier. He'd seemed fine. We'd had an argument about Stormzy. I'd offered to make him an Aperol Spritz and he'd said he was off the hard stuff. We'd done our annual Christmas quiz and he had been quizmaster. The only son out of seven siblings, he had helmed our family since Granddad died. So how could it be possible that he was no longer here? And even more important, how could he already be gone when life had been so unkind to him? When he had suffered so much? Things were supposed to get better; they were supposed to work out eventually. But they don't always—and they didn't for him. I fell apart. My whole family did. And then, mere weeks later, the world followed suit. A global pandemic changed the face of life as we knew it. Death, loss, and pain, unbearable pain, were all around us, everywhere we looked. I constantly searched over my shoulder, fearing it would happen again and reassuring myself that it couldn't. The worst had already come for me.

But then, in January 2021, as the third lockdown hung insidiously over our lives, the hardest one yet, I received a text in our group WhatsApp chat, apologizing for the medium and the message and letting us know that our friend Simon had died by suicide. I couldn't even ask the question "What?" this time. It was beyond all comprehension. I was silent. And somewhere deep, deep within me, I screamed. Inside I screamed for the minutes, hours, and days that followed. But I was locked in my house where I did not live alone and could not find peace, locked in my mind, which was knotted with the devastating anxiety of words that I understood on an in-tellectual level but could not believe to be true. And so I did not scream out loud, desperately as I wanted to, because I could not. I choked on my own sorrow and wondered how I would go on.

With no other option available to me in lockdown, I walked. Headphones in, India Arie soothing the thick, chok-ing feeling that consumed me. Right near my house was a lake. It looked mysterious and imposing but I was drawn to it and kept going back there. Instead of raw pain, when I was by the water I felt something closer to a simple numbness, which was a comfort and a reprieve. It started to feel like a holy place. I was in awe of it, although I didn't know why. And then one day I decided to get in.

It was freezing. Really and truly freezing. This was February and I didn't have any fancy equipment. Just my bra and underwear on that first day. I probably stayed in for less than a minute: just over to the buoy and back again. But as I gasped at the cold and struggled to mobilize my arms and legs like I'd been taught all those years ago—"breaststroke: arms, scooping round for ice cream; legs, bend, round, and snap together"—I realized that I had released something.

I became more proficient and adept, used to the temperature. As I started to swim more frequently and for longer, I began to shift the thick wedge that had lodged itself in my chest and my throat. It was as if each stroke, each splash, each gasp as I slid into the water loosened it a little each time. I started to feel freer, sometimes feeling waves of euphoria even though that *thing* still gripped my throat like a vise. And then, after some weeks of this routine, it dislodged itself completely. My body still followed the same mechanical motions—"bend, round, and snap together. Scooping up that ice cream"—but I started to cry.

I knew from that precise moment that I would be okay. Even as my cry became a bigger and uglier sob and I started to choke, exiting the water to hold on to something so that I wouldn't fall apart, I knew that it marked something monumental. My swimming turned from being an act that I didn't quite understand to something that was anchoring me, keeping me. But, despite the feeling that I had found something to hold on to—something truly worth bringing me out of bed each day—I saw nothing and no one to suggest that I would be able to share this journey with anyone. My hair was still a source of daily anxiety. There was no swimmer who looked like me at the lake. As far as I could tell, there was no swimmer who looked like me beyond the lake, either. In contrast to my many years as a competitive runner, where I felt as though I was born to chase my 1500-meter personal best, or travel to another new city and race another half marathon— where I was respected and admired—I had the distinct sense that I was an imposter in the swimming world. I realized very quickly that if I wanted to jump into the deep waters, I would have to be brave enough to do it alone.[1]

For every herd of elephants finding safety in the numbers of their tribe, there are those who travel solo, the very nature of their unique existence or presentation forcing them to go it alone. Mary Fields, or Stagecoach Mary, infamous as one of the toughest people of any gender in the American Wild West of the 1800s, is one such individual. She lived a life that defied expectations not only of her race but of her gender, too. Born an enslaved person, Mary moved to Mississippi after the Civil War, where she worked on riverboats and as a servant and laundress from time to time. From there, her life took a turn for the unconventional as she moved to live in a convent. Standing at over six feet tall and weighing more than two hundred pounds, she had a gruff voice and tough demeanor that set her apart from the convent's more docile nuns. She frequently swore, and having spent her earlier years working on riverboats drinking with men, the sedate life of the nunnery was firmly at odds with all that she had known up to that point. She began working as a groundskeeper and protected her beloved gardens with the ferocity of a tiger. One of the nuns allegedly stated: "God help anyone who walked on the lawn after Mary had cut it."[2] If this wasn't enough, Mary frequently took it upon herself to negotiate her wages with the nuns, behavior unheard of from any woman, let alone one who until recently had been enslaved and working entirely for free. Despite all of this, the unexpected happened: Mary Fields and Mother Mary Amadeus Dunne, the convent's Mother Superior, struck up a special and unique friendship. Some years later, when word reached the convent that Mother Mary had taken ill while away on mission, Mary Fields headed across the country to Montana to help nurse her back to health. She ended up staying out there with her in Cascade, Montana, until eventually news of her drinking, smoking, gun-carrying, and dressing in men's clothing reached the bishop. Finally, in 1894, after a standoff with a male colleague that involved both him and Fields pointing guns at each other, the bishop kicked her out of the convent for good.

For the first time in years, Fields was entirely alone—and accountable to no one. While many in her position would (understandably) have found any acceptable means of surviving that they could, Fields decided to eschew the acceptable and embrace solely the survival part. She made ends meet in any way possible: taking in laundry, taking on various domestic jobs, but also starting a number of businesses and gaining a reputation for being fond of hard liquor and partial to a gunfight or two. Just the usual then. She quickly became known as a maverick, someone society at the time had never seen before. And, before too long, her status as one of the toughest out there—afraid of nothing and no one, even of standing entirely alone—began to create opportunities for her. Just one year after being thrown out of the convent, at sixty-something years of age, she got a contract to become a star route carrier for the Post Office Department. Her role, whatever the weather and no matter how treacherous the terrain, was to deliver the mail, and to protect it from thieves and bandits along the way. Her guns would come in useful then. Perhaps unsurprisingly, this also made her the first African-American woman to work for the US postal service.

"Pioneer" is often an overused word, and perhaps not always given in the most deserving of circumstances, but Fields's work—and indeed her life—really does warrant this accolade. When delivering her mail each day, she carried two guns with her on her route: a rifle and a revolver. What's more, she did not hesitate to use them to protect herself and her precious cargo from whichever threat, human or animal, she encountered on her way, on one occasion even fending off an entire pack of wolves. Not only that, but she was dedicated, committed, and unerringly reliable, never missing a single day. If the snow was too deep, she would simply put the sacks on her shoulders and deliver the mail on snowshoes. On any other day, it was just Mary and her stagecoach, earning her the nickname that has stuck: Stagecoach Mary. Over time, she grew to be cherished by the residents of Cascade and, despite her tough exterior, greatly loved for her kindness to children.

In this way, Fields was something of a town hero for the next eight years that she safely delivered the mail each day. Whilst living such an unconventional life might typically have been her undoing, by simply following her own path, regardless of what anyone else thought, she actually carved out a space for herself where one might not have existed otherwise. By the time of her retirement, at around seventy years of age, Fields had won over the whole community. She found herself surrounded by free meals and constant companionship—an entire town even rallied to rebuild her house for her after a fire burned it down. She was so deeply loved that the town closed its schools every single year in honor of her birthday. When Montana introduced a new law banning women from entering bars, Fields was granted an exception by the mayor of Cascade. When she eventually died, her funeral was one of the largest that the town had ever seen.

Fields deserves her accolades as a pioneer at a time when paving any new route meant risking everything. It would be too easy to dismiss her story as one that belongs where it has mostly been left, gathering dust in the history books. However, Fields's thread in the tapestry is still being sewn and woven across the world for Black women. We are still all too frequently "the first," and this is not an easy label to wear. Women like Mary Fields or Diane Abbott, who walk paths no Black woman has ever stepped before, carry a weight that should not be theirs alone to bear. Perhaps we can help them to carry it.

In April 2022, Judge Ketanji Brown Jackson became the first Black woman to serve on the US Supreme Court. Jackson has degrees from Harvard University and Harvard Law School. She is one of the most qualified candidates in the history of the Supreme Court—no other candidate has held the roles of Supreme Court clerk, district judge, and public defender, and worked for the US Sentencing Commission. Despite her impeccable CV, her confirmation hearing was characterized by lines of questioning that had not been seen before. She was asked to define "woman," questioned on her thoughts on racism, continually interrupted as she coolly responded to questions that bordered on the ridiculous. Beyond the obvious insult that this questioning was to someone of Jackson's caliber, my heart also hurt from observing the dignity with which she simply accepted and calmly deflected it. When you are the first you do not just represent yourself. You represent every single person, past, present, and future, who looks like you. If you get it wrong, they get it wrong. The world will not let you forget it. Those coming after may never get another chance.

How then are we able to navigate being the first without allowing ourselves to become completely discredited, dehumanized, in the process? When we find ourselves alone in spaces, what might be useful to help us thrive? At precisely the same time as my swimming journey was taking place, preparations were underway for the 2021 Tokyo Olympics and history was about to be made. Alice Dearing was set to become the first Black woman to represent Great Britain as a swimmer at the Olympics. I could hardly take in the magnitude of this accomplishment. A young Black woman was about to go where nobody had gone before. Like Mary Fields before her, Dearing was set to move beyond the norms and the status quo of what Black women were considered capable of. I was still reeling from processing this and the excitement of beginning to follow Dearing's journey when FINA, the governing body for aquatic sports, banned the use of Soul Caps, a larger sized swimming hat specifically designed for Afro hair. Dearing, Afro very much intact, was about to change the narrative around the parameters of swimming as a Black woman, and FINA chose that moment to undercut everything that this history-making occasion represented. Worse, it was impossible to hear of FINA's actions without thinking that the ban was a message that Black people—and specifically Black women with more hair—did not belong.

Just as with Ketanji Brown Jackson, it seemed that the more the traditional power structures found themselves faced with a Black woman of unparalleled brilliance, the quicker they sought refuge in decisions that, whether they intended it or not, neutralized their efforts.

For one entire year, the ban remained. Black women did not belong in the swimming world. It was as simple as that. FINA apologized to Soul Cap, pledging to review their processes for all future applications and encouraging Soul Cap to reapply in the next submission window with FINA's full support, but the ban remained in place. Black women were shut out. Then, in September 2022, news broke that Soul Cap's swimming caps had been approved for competition. Finally, on a world stage, Black women were allowed to exist. Following further conversations with Soul Cap, FINA shared their Development Program Report, which outlined their $25.5 million investment into making swimming more accessible and inclusive across its 209 national member federations.[3]

Beyond all this, Dearing competed and made history. Not only did she forever show little Black and brown girls that there is a world of possibilities waiting for them and that there is nothing that they should not be able to try, she also went on to become an advocate for greater inclusion of Black people in aquatics, even founding the Black Swimming Association along the way. I have had the privilege of getting to meet and know her in recent months and she embodies the hope that will serve as a life raft to many who are lost at sea. We can write ourselves back into spaces, and in doing so, we make our mark and show those who come after that we belong—and we are not leaving.

Back in the nineteenth century, while Mary Fields was driving her stagecoach from Cascade, Montana, to St. Peter's Mission come rain or shine, one inspiring individual was embarking on a journey of her own. Mary McLeod Bethune was born in 1875 in a log cabin, the fifteenth of seventeen children. Like Hattie McDaniel, Mary Fields, and so many Black women before her, both of her parents were formerly enslaved people. At a young age, Bethune decided that the only difference between herself and white people was the ability to read and write. Inspired to learn and the only child in her family to go to school, she would go home each evening and teach her family what she had learned that day. She firmly believed that educating women and girls was key to improving the lives of Black people—and she went on to do so. She used $1.50 to found the Daytona Literary and Industrial Training School for Negro Girls, which started with just six students (five girls and her son, Albert). Word spread and she received donations in the form of cash equipment, and willing helping hands from local Black churches. Before she knew it, she had thirty girls at her school. Not satisfied with stopping there, she invited powerful white men to sit on her board of trustees, in a way that reminds me of Hattie McDaniel working with both Black and white people to ultimately get to where she wanted to be and Alice Dearing holding her own in a space where she stood truly alone.

So great are Bethune's achievements that it is hard not to sound like I am just listing them. She opened the first free library in Florida accessible to Black people, then the first hospital for African-American women. Then, after the Nineteenth Amendment was passed, which gave women the right to vote, she took this further and worked to help Black people make use of their right to vote. She launched a mass campaign promoting the importance of voting and worked to secure funding for those who couldn't afford to pay the poll tax. In 1935, around the same time that McDaniel was gaining traction as a Hollywood star, Bethune founded the National Council of Negro Women in New York City. This council united Black women from nearly thirty different organizations with the goal of working together to improve the lives of Black women across the state. She went on to become an educator, community organizer, public policy adviser, public health advocate, adviser to the president of the United States, and honorary general of the Women's Army for National Defense. And, as a final glorious detail, she walked around carrying a cane, not for support or because she needed it, but because she said it gave her "swank."

I often say "you can't be what you don't see" and I think this is just as relevant when talking about the first Black woman to work for the US postal service as it is when talking about the first Black woman swimmer to compete at the Olympics or to be elected to serve on the highest court in the land. These women are our heroes. Because of them, we can dream bigger. And yet, the consequences of not seeing ourselves in spaces and of holding that burden—that pressure of being the first—sometimes means that despite all the making, the breaking, and the shaping we can do, we are still forced to endure the unimaginable, even being faced with our very dignity being stripped from us. We cannot underestimate the cost for those who go first. They sacrificed enormously for us. We must not forget that. And yet, even so, I have heart. The "firsts" do not—cannot—ever truly stand alone, for they are woven into the tapestry that has come before. They are part of a bigger, brighter picture. And so I look for signs of the lemonade: the golden hue, the thread of gold. I was raised that way. Turn the bitterness of life into something sweet, refreshing, sustaining. I cling to that advice like a life raft when I feel myself drowning. So many of us know what it feels like to drown. To be choked deep inside by the thing in our chest, starved of oxygen by our own body. Let down by legs that will no longer allow us to stand. But we also know what it feels like to stand up again, fragile step by fragile step. We know what hope feels like.

For me, making lemonade is about hope. When you are caught in the heat, mouth in agony from desperate thirst, it is the promise of a sweet and refreshing drink that gets you through. The salvation is the lemonade, but it is the making of it that I am interested in. I started swimming because grief ripped me wide open, and whilst it may sound obvious, I really wasn't expecting it to. I wasn't expecting the agonizing gaping wound that choked me. I didn't expect to suddenly see my parents as fragile and frail. To go to bed at night and search the internet for answers to "What are the steps in a postmortem?" and "What happens when you die?"

I wasn't expecting to choke myself for air, certain that I could not survive this. I attempted one therapy session. It was very early 2020, right around the time of Uncle Delroy's death, and all I knew was that my response to grief did not feel normal. I could not see a way out of my pain. Desperate, I attempted a trial therapy session. As is becoming clearer now, though, I am an intensely private person. After two decades of not speaking and of holding everything in, it was very difficult to know where to begin. My thoughts would come in crisscrossing zigzags. The secrets I keep. The guilt I associate with physical intimacy. The consuming and overbearing fear that I and everyone I love will one day die. I did not possess words to articulate the reasons why I found myself in that therapy room. I felt that I could never explain myself in time. The therapist sprayed some incense and sounded her gong and I left more conflicted, more unsure, more silent than before.

And yet, in the process of trying to understand my grief, even if therapy did not work at that time, I decided I needed to step up on my own terms. Alongside starting swimming, I made a film, *Fifty-Four Days*, inspired by my experiences. The process of doing so was cathartic in itself, but since then it has now taken me around the world, its message of hope and healing after desperate loss clearly resonating with global audiences. I became mental health first-aid trained and learned about warning signs for those suffering from ill mental health. I became aware that men are most at risk of dying by suicide but also that Black women are more likely to live with anxiety and depression—and that they are likely to do this while caring for others, disproportionately carrying the burden and picking up the pieces. I also learned that Black people are disproportionately represented in mental health institutions, more likely to enter inpatient mental health services and be detained under the Mental Health Act than white people. According to research published in 2021 in the *Psychiatric Times*, Black women are only half as likely as white women to seek help.[4] From anxiety to depression to trauma to postnatal PTSD, Black women are 50 percent less likely to say, "I am struggling." Why does this discovery wound me quite as it does? Why does it take the breath out of my lungs? In my mind I run through my family, my friends, the people I know and love intimately. Taking the time to be less than okay is not something that particularly features. These statistics should not be surprising then—and yet they still are somehow, just because I cannot believe this is something that remains so widespread.

These alarming figures were previously attributed to stigma in the Black community around talking about mental health, but more recent research shows that stigma is not the main reason for Black women's hesitancy to seek help. While this might have been true twenty or thirty years ago, for those my age or even younger who have grown up with the internet and the constant iteration that we must "be kind" and "it's okay not to be okay," the idea of any real problem with stigma surrounding mental health does not make sense. In fact, the more I lose myself in the weighty and complex findings of psychologists' journals and reports, the more I discover something that really comes as no surprise at all. Our willingness to reach out and seek care, to raise our hand and say: "I am drowning, can you save me?," is most likely to be affected by our previous experience with institutions, medical practices, and mental health facilities. That means if we refer to a GP and are shut down we will close ourselves off in turn. I have no doubt that this happens across the board to people of all backgrounds, for who doesn't want to be believed when they share that they are in pain? Of course they might then think twice before sharing this again. Less common, however, is the fact that Black women may never see a clinician, doctor, or psychologist who looks like them. According to the American Psychiatric Association, Black clinicians represent only about 2 percent of practicing psychiatrists and 4 percent of psychologists providing care in the United States. I search the dusty crevices of my mind, trawling through GP visits, university welfare officers, travel vaccinations, and any form of institutional interaction I have had where I might have felt able to reach out and say: "I am scared." I have never met with a Black representative in any of these institutions. Never.

What does this actually mean? Well, we would hope against all hopes that the ability of the trained professionals to do the job they have spent years learning how to do would override any sort of bias or even simple trust processes, and in many cases, of course, this is true. However, it is not the case every time. This means that often those who do present and seek care can be misdiagnosed, not due to any malice but simply due to a fundamental misunderstanding. What about if we take as an example a Black woman who felt affected by the killing of Breonna Taylor? This woman might have seen herself in Breonna's position, knowing that it very well could have been her, and consequently presented with anxiety. For a clinician with no experience of what living with this sort of anxiety means, they may misdiagnose, attributing a clinical diagnosis to a cultural illness. The wrong treatment could be prescribed, or maybe even nothing at all; a gaping void in the place of talking therapy or sleeping pills, or a casual overlooking of a manageable mental illness, leading to devastating consequences that could have been foreseen.

Since my unsuccessful encounter with therapy I have reflected a lot on my own internal biases. I do not want or need to perpetuate any stereotypes about Black women "coping." I want to be part of an entire movement of women who speak up and out when things hurt, who don't stay choking in the deep end of the water knowing that they cannot swim. My sister is currently completing her master's degree in the psychology of mental health and well-being, and works as a trailblazing support across the West End and more recently on my film sets too, pioneering a role that never existed before. The feedback she gets from this—from the simple fact of people seeing a Black woman in these spaces, holding space, is inspiring in itself. More than that, though, I think I can recognize that "therapy" comes in a number of forms. Maybe there are ways to save ourselves from drowning that we haven't yet considered and maybe that form for me looks a little like jumping into a cold lake or asking fifty Black women to tell me what they find beautiful about themselves. Perhaps instead when we feel like we are sinking and don't know what to do, the way to help ourselves is as simple as just lying back and letting ourselves float. This thought allows me to recognize how Alice Dearing's thread is linked enduringly to mine and to Michaela Coel's before us: If we lie there in the water and just let ourselves *be*, who knows what we might find in the silence.

Often, when we do so, no matter how alone we feel, someone unexpected might just be throwing us the life raft. Like the residents of Cascade, Montana, who unexpectedly rallied around Stagecoach Mary, or the outraged general public who protested FINA's ban of an inclusive swimming cap brand, lifting Dearing in their arms as they did so, these women are woven into the tapestry, too.

Even though it often seems that standing alone is the only

option, allyship is important. It really matters. Not only that, but seeing people we relate to in spaces we exist in is important. In fact, it is more than important: It is life-changing and potentially life-saving. Whilst considering this, I come back to my own experience as a little girl with an Afro who wanted to swim. Perhaps stopping swimming when I'd been good at it wasn't just teenage vanity or boredom. Perhaps it was my being pushed out of a space where I didn't belong because nobody looked like me, nor had they ever thought to make space for anyone who did. Maybe all it would have taken was for someone to say, "Come on! Keep going!" There is a need for this. According to Swim England, 95 percent of Black adults and 80 percent of Black children in England do not swim. One in four Black children leave primary school not knowing how to swim. These facts both terrify and anger me. Being able to access a lake every day in the aftermath of my grief not only healed me, it saved me. Swimming should not be inaccessible to Black people or working-class people or any group at all. Dearing has gone forth now; she has been "the first." I hope—real hope deep in the core of my chest where my grief used to choke me—that she will not be the last. Pioneers, come forth.

So, drowning. There is a lot to be said for simply protecting your own space. Knowing when you will be available for people to approach you and knowing when your time is your own. Knowing when you can support others and knowing when you just need to take a moment to support yourself. You don't have to help everyone. There is a lot to be said for recognizing that perhaps spending the rest of your life in a convent doesn't work for you. That you are more comfortable holding the reins of a stagecoach than a baby—or that while all your friends are out partying you would rather be at the pool, focusing on your strokes and honing your breathing. If we feel like we are lost, choking on the thing in our chests, then we can just pause. Hope lives and breathes in many different forms. An extended hand, a trailblazing Black woman, a quietly accomplished individual helping others to help themselves. Or, sometimes, hope lives and breathes in stillness and in silence and in accepting but not being overwhelmed by the panic. Hope is the word.

Mary Fields and Mary McLeod Bethune share more than a first name. They never really did what was expected of them, and they certainly refused to be put in a box. There is a lot that we can learn from them today, in not overlooking anyone and bringing others up with us. Just like Michaela Coel, we can lean into a respect for the choice of an individual to embrace silence, even encouraging them to find it when they are being drowned out. More than anything, though, women such as Alice Dearing, Ketanji Brown Jackson, Mary Fields, and Mary McLeod Bethune teach us that the world will not always make a space for us, and if we wait for it to do so we will always do ourselves a disservice, numb at the edge of the water. Zooming out and applying this on a wider scale, it is our duty to fight to keep this hope alive with the spirit of these women who created the blueprint. Only by doing this will we ever really allow for a diverse range of perspectives that come from furious, glorious, fully realized human beings—with a whole lot of swank.

Part III

RESILIENCE

*In which we illuminate Black women's
continuous capacity to rise*

Chapter Eight

GRANDMOTHER

I HAD MY UPS AND downs, but I always found the inner strength to pull myself up. I was served lemons, but I made lemonade."[1]

Hattie White, Beyoncé's grandmother-in-law, surrounded by family and friends at her ninetieth birthday, declares these words to rapturous applause. As she speaks, underscored by a delicate strings solo, we see women—Black women of all ages, appearances, and walks of life. The camera slowly pans from a little girl, Afro resplendent as she runs across the grass before moving back to the home video and Hattie's speech as the room erupts into cheers. Each individual there recognizes the hardships that life has given to this Black woman. They know it is their story, too. The home video cuts to young Black women collecting fruit and vegetables: a visual emblematizing of growth and new life. The next frame is a striking tableau. Seven Black women sit facing the viewer, a shot that is held unflinchingly for ten entire seconds, daring anyone to challenge this defiant and resilient statement of power. "Redemption," the final chapter of Beyoncé's recipe, brings together each ingredient in potent and perfect formation. Rising out of the depths of life's hardships, *Lemonade* invites us to watch and be watched by Serena Williams, dancing unapologetically as she asserts her Blackness and her womanhood. It invites us to consider Leah Chase, Zendaya, Quvenzhané Wallis, and, unflinchingly, to face Lesley McSpadden, Sybrina Fulton, Wanda Johnson, and Gwen Carr, mothers of Mike Brown, Trayvon Martin, Oscar Grant, and Eric Garner, respectively. It calls for us to take up more space, to get in formation and recognize the importance of this matrilineal connection between generations of Black women.

The end tableau of seven Black women and Beyoncé's call for a united "formation" throughout *Lemonade* is a marker of time for me: where we have come from and how far we have to go. It is a beautiful tapestry, there is no mistaking that; but it is more than this. It has depth, richness, and color still to be woven into it. Many threads and strands are yet to be added. We are only partway through the crafting of the tapestry that connects past, present, and future, and we must engage actively, consciously, and profoundly with the weaving of our stories. The tapestry will become our comfort and our weapon, our means of forming identity across the divide and rewriting narratives that have excluded Black women from their scope.

How do we achieve this? We bring our grandmothers close and yet we hold our own selves up to the light next to them. As that little girl discovered at the hairdressing salon: We are enough.

Ena. My grandmother. She is the closest link to my past, to the island I come from. If someone took a camera and every ten years decided to capture a moment in time, or take oils to paper, or paint to a canvas, they would conjure a singular defining image. The first would be my nan's house in Newport, South Wales. Everything feels as though it centers around this tiny townhouse. It's funny how it's just bricks. One day they won't even be there. Or maybe they will outlast us all. You could start with baby me, in a Moses basket. My nan would be in the kitchen, feeding forty of us from one minuscule oven. She might still be wearing her nurse's uniform— her superhero's cape—coming from or going to her next shift, never complaining about the forty miles she traveled by bus each day to fulfill her promise to herself of dedicating her life to the National Health Service if they gave her a job. My granddad would be sitting in his chair in the living room, regaling the room with stories, citing some of his still-quoted wisdom.

Ten years into the future and it would no longer just be me but my two sisters, too. We would be an unbreakable, unshakable trio that even the deepest of rifts in a sticky, sweaty Soho pub on a summer's day twenty years later couldn't separate. We would be dancing and performing shows, our granddad sitting back and listening to us now, or maybe watching his beloved QVC, much adored for the simple reason that it had no violence. My nan would still be in that kitchen. I can smell the rice and peas, the curried goat that I never ate as by ten I had already decided that meat was murder. Eventually, my nan would come in, and she might dance with us, laughing at our endless energy.

The portrait ten years after that would be stiller, quieter. Granddad's chair empty now. The vision of my nan clutching his hand for the last time as we sang him on his way out of this earth is seared into my mind forever. It doesn't feel quiet. "Goodbye, Gerald," she called over the singing and the crying and the noise that accompanies death in our culture, as she held that hand and didn't let go. The hundreds of mourners at the church heard and saw in that simple phrase the breadth of a relationship that had seen two young lovers leave the island that they called home and slowly send for their six children one by one, paving new life from old.

The portrait ten years after that is still being painted, but I think it would center on my nan. She has her own chair now. She can still often be found in the kitchen, but also just as likely out at church. She is more stubborn, less likely to do something she doesn't want to. I understand this, like it even. In this portrait you might find me sitting at her feet, just as I did in my Moses basket all those years earlier. It's different now, though. I want to listen, I want to observe. I want to weave the tapestry with her.

The deeper we dive into the legacies of our grandmothers the more it becomes apparent that we do not know enough. We could never know enough. There is that funny old saying, "You can't teach your grandmother to suck eggs," and while I take the warning and respect my elders, there is also a curious sense of rebellion in me. Might we not have something to share? Might we not have as much to offer them as we have to learn? There is both a relief and a tension in seeing that our foremothers have already walked our path—comfort in a route already paved—but a challenge in the compulsion to go further, to make progress. If our greatest goal is to honor their legacy, then how better to do so than to take up where they left off, being brave enough to try to forge our own path without being swallowed whole by the possibility of failure? How better to do so than to dare to place ourselves in line with their story?

With my nan there is a sense of "been there done that," a quiet knowledge of the life she has led, the storms she has weathered. She did not always get her dues. The threads in her part of the tapestry are tattered. Sitting at her feet I start to think about how I might help to dust this tapestry off, an archaeologist performing a delicate excavation. Even more than that, though, perhaps in making our own additions to the tapestry we discover the role that we play. Maybe our excavation plays a part in a great exultation, shining a light on the stories that our grandmothers never told us but the world deserves to know. Maybe our shine can also increase the value of the tapestry, enhancing it and making clear for all to see that we have as much to add as we have to learn.

We all know about Rosa Parks. She was a hero in her own right. Her story is legendary: On Thursday, December 1, 1955, she boarded a bus after a long day at work and headed for home. Three stops went by before it started to get busy and as white passengers began to fill the aisles, the driver asked the Black passengers to move to the back of the bus so that the white people could sit down. All but one—Rosa Parks—agreed. Parks, quite simply, was tired. Her one word—no—set a chain of events in motion, leading to the Montgomery bus boycott, the civil rights movement, and the emergence of leaders such as Martin Luther King Jr., at the time of Parks's protest still an unknown preacher. Parks was held up—heralded even—as the innocent victim of a racial apartheid, the brave saint who dared to say no. None of this was entirely true. Parks might well have been an innocent seamstress, but she was also a long-standing fierce feminist and political activist. Even more crucially, she was not the first person to refuse to give up her seat on a bus. That honor goes to fifteen-year-old Claudette Colvin, who just nine months earlier in the very same town had also taken her stand. This time, it was March 2, 1955, and school had closed early. Colvin and her friends were on the bus traveling home, sitting at the back in their segregated section. As the bus began to fill up the driver asked Colvin and her friends to move to allow for a white woman to sit—a request for four young Black women to stand so that one white woman could sit. In Colvin's own words: "He wanted me to give up my seat for a white person and I would have done it for an elderly person but this was a young white woman. Three of the students had got up reluctantly and I remained sitting next to the window."[2]

Just like Parks after her, Colvin cited her constitutional right to stay sitting, pointing to the fare she had paid, and refused to move. She later spoke about her inspirations and immovable strength to hold firm to her convictions coming from the likes of great abolitionists and warrior women. "Whenever people ask me: 'Why didn't you get up when the bus driver asked you?' I say it felt as though Harriet Tubman's* hands were pushing me down on one shoulder and Sojourner Truth's† hands were pushing me down on the other shoulder. I felt inspired by these women because my teacher taught us

---

* Harriet Tubman was an escaped enslaved woman, nurse, suffrage supporter, and abolitionist who became a conductor on the Underground Railroad, helping to lead enslaved people to freedom.

† Sojourner Truth was an abolitionist, activist, and author who was born into slavery but escaped to her freedom in 1826, going on to publish her well-known speech with the refrain "Ain't I a Woman?"

about them in so much detail."[3] This points to an element of Colvin's personality that has since been glossed over. She was intelligent, studious even. One of her schoolmates described her as a "bookworm . . . always studying and using long words."[4] In tenth grade, when Colvin's teacher asked the class to write down what they wanted to be when they grew up, Colvin unfurled her paper to reveal the words "President of the United States."

So this was the young woman who refused to get up from her seat. The driver called the police, who called her the N-word as his colleague made a joke about Colvin's bra size. Then, they dragged her off the bus and beat her. "I was really afraid, because you just didn't know what white people might do at that time," Colvin told an interviewer. "I didn't know if they were crazy, if they were going to take me to a Klan meeting. I started protecting my crotch. I was afraid they might rape me."[5] It was only five months later, in August of that same year, that fourteen-year-old Emmett Till was pulled out of a local river, having been abducted, tortured, and brutally murdered for allegedly whistling at a white woman in a store. It was an unspeakable act of barbarity, never met with justice, that is no less distressing today. So the fear of repercussions—of torture or even death—were real for Colvin.

As word of the unfolding storm began to spread, the leaders of the civil rights movement began to gather. Colvin had brought the revolution to Montgomery, Alabama. However, as her trial got underway, it became apparent that she was not going to become the face of the movement. Despite refusing to give up her seat nine months before Rosa Parks, her story was buried and has been all but forgotten. Why didn't Colvin gain the credit she so rightfully deserved? There is not really any one easy explanation for this. Colvin thinks that Parks had the right image to become the face of resistance for a number of reasons. Parks had already worked before with the NAACP. Perhaps this familiarity made her a safer option. There is also the possibility that the organization didn't want a teenager in the role, a sense that life experience might be essential to become a leader, an unfair dismissal of the many skills or talents that a younger individual could bring. Making this worse, as Colvin's trial began to gain prominence, she fell pregnant, a deadly sin for an unmarried teenager at the time—and the fact that the child was born out of what Colvin herself called "statutory rape" entirely overlooked. "If the white press got ahold of that information, they would have [had] a field day," said Rosa Parks. "They'd call her a bad girl, and her case wouldn't have a chance."[6] In Colvin's words: "They said they didn't want to use a pregnant teenager because it would be controversial and the people would talk about the pregnancy more than the boycott."[7] There are no surprises there, but imagine the groundbreaking conversation that could have happened had there been a greater capacity for an intergenerational dialogue. Making space for these dialogues to exist and to thrive is vital, as is communicating across genders and across many strands of existences. We stand to lose out on so much if we don't open up our communication channels in this way.

More than just the pregnancy, though, Colvin was from an impoverished part of town that the Black middle classes looked down on. In contrast, Parks was middle class, educated, and—crucially—light skinned. Even though Colvin's actions came first, she was a dark-skinned Black woman and this counted against her. Colvin herself stated that she did not believe her pregnancy was the only contributing factor in her dismissal: "It would have been different if I hadn't been pregnant, but if I had lived in a different place or been light-skinned, it would have made a difference, too. They would have come and seen my parents and found me someone to marry."[8] Gwen Patton, a civil rights activist in Montgomery since the 1960s, agrees: "It was partly because of her color and because she was from the working poor. . . . She lived in a little shack. It was a case of 'bourgey' Blacks looking down on the working-class Blacks."[9] This is a sobering reality check. Colorism is a direct by-product of the existing power structures. As a beneficiary myself of the privilege that accompanies those with lighter skin, I see responsibility to acknowledge this—and call it out. The same applies for those who come from class privilege or any other sort of background that provides an advantage. Claudette Colvin is the living, breathing reality of the consequences of not doing so.

We must consider how, just as Rosa Parks was not the first person to give up her seat on the bus, so too can history be presented in a way that may not be the definitive version. Often, the dominant narrative holds many dazzling threads beneath it, just waiting to be unpicked. By seeing ourselves in this thread of gold, by taking on the role of excavator, we can actually participate in bringing it to light for the first time. This one is for the grandmothers.

When *Empire Windrush* docked at Tilbury on June 22, 1948, a new dawn was born for many. This marked a significant moment in British history: At the request of the monarch, the ship carried one of the first large groups of postwar West Indian immigrants to the United Kingdom, and this event has become symbolic of the generation of Commonwealth citizens who came to live in Britain after World War II, helping to rebuild the country and build their own legacy as they went. Carrying 1,027 passengers, the ship had set sail on a voyage from the Caribbean to London, transporting individuals to the promise of a new life, whether they were coming to work, to study, or to help bring Britain back to life. According to records held within the British Library, of the 257 female passengers, 188 of them were traveling alone, from all over the Caribbean. History has prioritized the stories of the men coming over on the *Empire Windrush* to help make England what it is, but the stories of the women remain conspicuously absent. I traced their names in the passenger list: Rosemary Lewis with two-year-old Jessica. Suzanne and Marie Berger, setting sail from Jamaica, aged one and four—seemingly without their parents. Even eighty-year-old

Gertrude Whitelaw from Kingston, traveling without her husband. What has happened to the stories of these women? What became of them? Diving deep into the passenger lists told me that there were a number of reasons for their absence; some were solely practical, including the fact that for women, this trip was significantly more expensive than it was for men. Men could purchase a special £28 ticket because they could travel in a shared space at the bottom of the ship, but this was seen as improper for women, whose tickets were a considerably more costly £43.

Beyond these tales of practicalities and finances, though, I wanted to know more of the lives of the women. Just like Claudette Colvin, they have fallen through the crevices of history. The stories that have been most told and most documented are of the men: smart suits and shiny eyes. In reality, the women were right there with them, sometimes in the most unconventional of ways.

Twenty-one-year-old Trinidadian Mona Baptiste was one such woman. On the passenger record she was listed as a clerk, but already being a relatively well-known blues singer back in the Caribbean, she took a chance, pursued her dream to travel Europe, and went on to have a successful career as a singer in Germany. When we imagine fresh starts we often think of wide-eyed teenagers, their lives stretching out in front of them. In fact, the more I study the passenger records, the more I trace the shape of "grandmother." Many of the passengers are in their fifties, sixties, seventies—even eighties, in the case of Gertrude Whitelaw, traveling alone thousands of miles to a new life. I think again of my own grandparents, who came over in their twenties and sent for their children one by one. My mum was the last child to actually be born in Jamaica and she was raised by her grandmother Beatrice until my grandparents could afford to send for her.

I am intrigued by the women on the boat, by their audacity, their tenacity. And the more I read the more certain I become that these are the right words to describe one such passenger. Evelyn Wauchope was a dressmaker in her mid- to late twenties who, against all odds, became something of a legend, gaining notoriety for stowing away—an act of unprecedented bravery that would have required blackmail, bravado, and a real sense of adventure. When her fellow passengers eventually found her hiding at the bottom of the ship they were so impressed and charmed by her risky act that they clubbed together to pay for her ticket, ensuring that she would not be punished or imprisoned. One of the ship's passengers wrote: "A couple of English and Jamaican cabin passengers . . . decided that they simply could not let this adventurous woman be imprisoned on arrival in England." The penalty was up to twenty-eight days. "Everyone was sympathetic . . . Delroy Stevens and the Calypso singers got together, and gave a benefit concert."[10] They made enough for her ticket plus £4 pocket money. Evelyn Wauchope flirted with danger and she won. I feel a searing connection to this woman, who was the same age I am now when she stowed away and, I learn, died on May 20—my own birthday.

These connections are not coincidences. We are meant to see ourselves in our grandmothers' eyes. They are the great oak but we are the seedlings, rooting ourselves and growing in stature every single day by their sides.

I begin to unlearn—or relearn—my own assumed knowledge. There is no logic or reason to who gets remembered or why. Even my discoveries of Claudia Jones founding Carnival are proven to be only partly true. I find that the Notting Hill Carnival has another unsung hero: Rhaune Laslett. With very early aims of encouraging the many cultural groups of the Notting Hill community to get to know each other a little and to counteract the presiding image of Notting Hill being essentially nothing more than a slum, community activist Laslett had a vision of a celebratory street fair, known then as the Notting Hill Fair. In an interview with *The Grove* (the newsletter of the London Free School that Laslett co-founded), she said: "We felt that although West Indians, Africans, Irish and many other nationalities all live in a very congested area, there is very little communication between us. If we can infect them with a desire to participate then this can only have good results."[11] Starting on September 18, 1966, a melting pot of culture and community was born. The music ranged from Afro-Cuban to Irish dancing, with marching bands and steel bands coming together and costumes hired from Madame Tussauds and the entire parade being followed by fire engines. Carnival lingers in its color and its community.

Why did Laslett not get her dues? As a half–Indigenous American, half-Russian social worker, perhaps she didn't fit the convenient picture. Yet without her, Carnival as we know it today would not exist. As Black women, or white women, or nonbinary people, or men—whoever we are, we have a responsibility to refuse to allow narratives to shift in favor of who fits the most convenient story. We will never fully weave our tapestry if we approach it with threads already missing— or threads we are choosing to ignore. The single story must continue to be shattered.

Diving deeper and in a more nuanced way, pockets of communities who have been overlooked exist in almost any direction we care to look and Black women can be found nestled within most of them. East London is one of those pocketed communities with precious few stories of our grandmothers existing in the archives. Kathleen Wrasama is one woman I manage to find. She was born in Ethiopia in the early twentieth century and was taken to England by missionaries as a young girl in 1917. From what might have been a tragic end, she found a home in the Somali sailors' community of East London and went on to live a rich and distinct life, even taking on the role of an extra in films with Paul Robeson just before the Second World War. Later, she established a Black seamen's mission in Stepney, East London, and went on to found the Stepney Coloured People's Association, an organization working to improve education and housing prospects for Black people. She created a space of community for Black people at a time when this just didn't exist.

Maybe this is it: Maybe this is what our grandmothers did for us. Maybe the debt that they laid down was quite simply to create a space. Maybe, in fact, all along there has been a plan, a form of control in every single narrative that seems to have been overlooked. I come back once again to the revelation I found in Michaela Coel's invocation to simply see what comes to you in the silence—or my own mum's call to let the peace of God reign. Maybe these women have been giving me the clues that our grandmothers had already passed down and in embracing a silence of my own I am simply discovering a new way of finding my joy, forging my path.

Now, though, thinking of my grandmother—quiet through all those years but bursting with stories of a life well lived, worlds created, plans made—and seeing that there is often so much more to any story than meets the eye, I sit again with the silence. I probe deeper. What if we see the silence of our grandmothers, the stories overlooked, as having a life of their own? What if this silence is actually alive, contributing to the tapestry? I think of the times in my own life when silence has been permitted to shine its light in this way; when silence becomes a plan or an active choice, executed with rigor. Rather than criticizing or dismissing the silence and absence of our grandmothers from our narratives, perhaps we should look a little closer, listen a little harder, and see what it might point to. Maybe silence is a form of protection against a world that refuses to listen. In this context silence can be an actively chosen and powerful form of resistance. Silent protests such as the 1968 Olympics Black Power salute, where two African-American athletes raised a black-gloved fist during the playing of the US national anthem, have historically been used as a compelling means of fighting against oppression in a way that words cannot.

There are nuances to silence, though. Some voices inevitably speak louder than others. In her book *Surviving the Silence*, Charlotte Pierce-Baker writes about her journey of healing after experiencing rape, drawing upon the double bind that Black women face, describing how "for Black women, where rape is concerned, race has preceded issues of gender. We are taught that we are first Black, then women."[12] Pierce-Baker describes how particularly in cases involving Black men raping Black women, Black women have opted for silence, not just because they are ashamed, but also as a means of protecting the image of Black people worldwide. Speaking out following her rape at the hands of two Black men, Pierce-Baker described how she didn't want to taint the perception of Black men to her young Black son or to her white neighbors and so she quite simply kept quiet about what had happened to her: "I didn't want to confirm the white belief that all Black men rape . . . I assumed silent responsibility for the infamy of others."[13] Again, this makes me think of Ketanji Brown

Jackson's dignified silence in the face of undignified questioning. Being a grandmother, being "the first," is to protect.

Pierce-Baker speaks of the fear that she felt in the months and years following her rape, which translated directly into a refusal to identify the perpetrators: "If I identify him, I condemn him. I would have to point and say 'That one.' I did not want that kind of power to condemn a Black man, any man." Silence here is both a survival instinct and a fiercely protective measure.

The grandmothers are responsible for the survival of an entire race, carrying the world on their shoulders. This has to end. And yet, a consideration of what speaking out might actually mean for Black women makes me stop and consider. I understand. Pierce-Baker points to the future generations of young Black men who will continue to be profiled as rapists or criminals, a stifling and silencing of opportunities for them. Maybe, just as in the eyes of the NAACP Colvin's pregnancy would have reflected badly on the movement, so too could reporting a crime committed by a Black man negatively affect perceptions of Black women, already positioned as sexualized bodies unworthy of love. There is a pervasive and profound fear that is echoed repeatedly throughout the interviews that Pierce-Baker conducts with other survivors, where she reflects on what exactly it might mean for her own son if she sends a Black man to jail. Even within the midst of their own oppression, Black women adopt responsibility for the entirety of their race, a silent sacrifice for the protection of others.

However, according to recent statistics, this silence of Black women is born out of more than just protection of others within their race. Black women are still less likely to report being raped or sexually assaulted than white women, even if they are not attacked by a Black man. Of the successful prosecutions and reportings that do exist, the stories rarely belong to Black women. According to *Forbes*, the Department of Justice in the United States estimates that for every white woman who reports her rape, at least five white women do not; and yet, for every African-American woman who reports her rape, at least fifteen African-American women do not report theirs.[14]

Pierce-Baker describes speaking with a male ally who states that Black women "are the survivors of a crime that doesn't exist." But again by challenging myself to learn, unlearn, and relearn, perhaps this can be reinterpreted. Maybe silence here becomes a form of resistance and support from within the Black community. And if not that, maybe in respecting the choice of an individual, an actively chosen silence resists any definite reading and therefore becomes in and of itself a deed of defiantly active resistance. Maybe, out of the silence, we are creating new identities for ourselves as survivors. Through the creation of a support network of victims drawn together by simply speaking to Pierce-Baker—and agreeing to have their stories published—these Black women are existing in silence no more. They may not have sent the perpetrator of their most horrific crime to jail, but they have acknowledged that this cannot happen again. The silence is shattered.

I see this again and again throughout history: our foremothers bearing arms so that we might walk freely, and the relationship between Black men and women in particular is one where difficult decisions have frequently had to be made. As the Black liberation movements of the sixties and seventies grew, Black women began to query their role in these movements—and what the role of people of different genders could and should look like. Within movements such as the Black Panthers, women began to feel undermined, sexualized, or simply dismissed. They didn't get much say in organizational matters and similarly didn't feel able to challenge their perceived place. Splinter groups began to emerge, inspired by movements from women in countries such as Zimbabwe and Mozambique. One of the first and possibly most prolific of these groups was the Brixton Black Women's Group, established in 1973 by a collective of women including fellow Panthers and revolutionary women Olive Morris, Beverley Bryan, and Liz Obi. On the whole, the movements where the founding members of the Brixton Black Women's Group had come from, such as the Black Panthers, were already besieged by problems, but it was the women who were immediately accused of causing the ruptures. They didn't see it that way; they were simply searching for a movement that related specifically to issues that affected them, that saw them as equals and comrades in arms. By forming the Brixton

Black Women's Group, they were setting their own precedent, forming a collective that was different from both the Black liberation and white feminist movements. The movement was their own. Their track record was impressive. They campaigned against police harassment, mobilized the Brixton community against the scores of empty houses, and helped campaign for parental rights. Olive Morris was heavily involved with the movement campaigning for squatters' rights and found the movement's headquarters by simply commandeering a space. When the council threatened to evict them, Morris climbed onto the roof, refusing to come down until they surrendered the building. Continuing the weaving of the tapestry and interconnected threads, this building went on to become the Sabarr bookshop, one of the first Black-owned bookshops in South London. Even more inspiring than finding their space through alternative means and their ethos, these women also found a way of operating that held true to their roots. When protesting or trying to stand off against anything that would involve police threats, they would form solid groups and stand united, strength in trusted revolutionary numbers. Beverley Bryan stated that: "They were less likely to arrest a group of women, especially if they had their children with them. I remember at one picket there was a baby."[15]

They were radical, in the way that our grandmothers often are, and were a collective in the truest sense of the word, even publishing a book as a unit exploring the struggles of

Black women in Britain. What a joy it is to be writing words now that speak to their legacy.

Bryan discussed this in an interview, encouraging others—like me—to put pen to paper. Responding to a question about why Black women have been overlooked, she referred to the African proverb "The lion's story will never be told by the hunters," challenging anyone reading to tell their own story and not wait for it to be told by the more powerful voice. Through her own work as an educator, Bryan clearly thought about *how* things could become more effective: She strategized and this was to the great advantage of everyone around her—and all those who came after her. One of her accomplishments was working to decolonize the curriculum way before this became a catchy phrase bandied about on social media. She worked as a teacher and upon realizing one year that her class was majority Black she began to think carefully about how to best serve that community. One thing she knew from the start was that her teaching would be entirely centered on making her students feel proud of their background. Just as Claudette Colvin had channeled Sojourner Truth and Harriet Tubman thanks to the dedication of her teacher, so too would Bryan's students know from whence they came. "I wanted to give my students a kind of self-defense against the negativity they would encounter," Bryan says. "I wanted to give them Black stories, Black culture and Black history as a way of affirming that you come from a history of proud people."[16] There is such a sense of joy for me in seeing our foremothers share stories of their foremothers. So they too knew how much we stood to learn. I think it is also a testament to the power of teaching, a still undervalued profession. Students don't forget these lessons from their teachers. Bryan lives in Jamaica now but says that when she comes back to visit London she will often bump into old pupils who are quick to comment on her work to diversify the curriculum and declare: "You were doing these things back in the day, Miss!"[17]

I think it's also interesting that Bryan wanted to create a Black curriculum as a form of defense. In my mind it goes way beyond this. For me, what Bryan does is not just to fight the case for the importance of sharing stories of Black historical figures, but also to provide a celebration of their work and of their lives and to center our own as being a continuation of the story. In her own words: "If people called you names, rather than say: 'I'm not Black,' you could point to what Black people had achieved."[18] I love that. It is not about shying away from who we are, but rather arming ourselves with the knowledge of what our people have done and how we now deserve to take our rightful stance.

There is a Gullah proverb:

Ef oona ent kno weh oona da gwine, oona should kno weh oona come from.

Its English translation is something like:

If you don't know where you are going, you should know where you come from.

We may not know where we are going—in fact, it may change every single day—but we can and should take comfort in the women who hold our history in their hands, keeping it safe for when we are ready, waiting for when we might need it. It is thanks to the women who came before—our grandmothers—that we know where we come from, thanks to them that we can build upward and outward, thanks to them that we can hold our heads high, skyward to the stars and out to the sea, as we continue to pull tight the thread that forms our glittering trail of gold.

Chapter Nine

MOTHER

I READ SOMETHING THE OTHER day: *It takes a village to raise a mother, too.* That floored me. Becoming a mother does not automatically mean that you stop being a woman. It does not automatically mean that you know all the answers. It does not even automatically mean that you want to be in the role of carer, nurturer, giver of life. Sometimes motherhood requires more than a person is able to give. Sometimes motherhood is the ultimate sacrifice, and the sacrificial lamb in question is not willing or able. And sometimes, motherhood is simply a daily battle, a daily struggle, a daily need to demonstrate or at least to find somewhere deep within a resilience that surpasses all patience and understanding.

If our grandmothers show us where we come from, then our mothers show us something of the making and the remaking we are doing now as we navigate our space and place.

If our grandmothers teach us how to resist and to become, our mothers teach us how to make and how to do. When I think of our mothers, I think of founders, shakers, people who faced the worst and came out the other side intact. Maybe not smiling, maybe not even thriving. But they lived to tell the tale.

I once attended a talk at the Oxford Union. It was on Black Lives Matter, before its major resurgence in 2020. The panelists included Sybrina Fulton, Geneva Reed-Veal, Valerie Bell, and Gwen Carr, mothers of Trayvon Martin, Sandra Bland, Sean Bell, and Eric Garner, respectively. Before I even arrived in those hallowed halls—the first time I had ever set foot in the Oxford Union—I knew that it was going to be a monumental evening. I was going to see the mothers of these individuals I had seen in the papers, on my television, all over my news feed. I knew that they were integral to the movement; I just didn't fully understand how.

Truth is a subjective thing. Who is to say what is real and what is not? Truth changes, shifts, transmutes, translates, depending on who holds it in their hands. However, there are some immutable, immovable facts. One of these facts is quite simple: No mother should have to bury a child. The very laws of nature dictate that a child should, in any normal sense of how things operate, outlive their parent. Beyond that, though, when a woman has carried a child for nine months, kept them alive from within the safety of her own body, she should not have to outlive that child. She should not lose that child to illness, to a car crash, to a freak lightning strike, or to a climbing accident. And what is nonnegotiable, beyond every conceivable way that a mother might lose her child, is that she should never lose her baby at the hands of a police officer shooting them like a dog or squeezing the air out of their lungs. That, for me, is an immutable, immovable truth.

As the discussion at the Oxford Union went on, and we began to hear the impassioned words of these women—these mothers—I was hit with one simple fact: I had never considered the mothers before. I could tell you every single way that their children died: chokehold, shooting, hanging in her jail cell, shooting, chokehold, knee on the neck . . . The list goes on, it goes on and it will go on even beyond the words that I write today. I know the ages at which their children were killed. I know their education background, the siblings they have, the nuances of their trials. And yet I do not know anything about the women who gave them life.

I can hardly breathe. I sit at the Oxford Union, barely still on my seat because it is all I can do to stay sitting when every single part of me wants to shout—or scream. And all around me, people are starting to break down. They are crying, literally sobbing at the testimonies of these mothers who faced the ultimate injustice, for whom the self-evident truth that no mother should bury a child was ignored. Worse, it was ignored by those who had sworn to protect. DeRay Mckesson, an American civil rights activist and educator, is also on the panel and he opens by stating one simple sentence: "Protest at its root is telling the truth in public." I guess then I am protesting. I am screaming as loud as I can that no parent should ever lose their child in this way.

The Black Lives Matter movement was built by women. In the wake of the killing of Trayvon Martin, shot in the street as he walked home from buying sweets and a watermelon drink, and the subsequent acquittal of his killer, a new hashtag started by three women, Alicia Garza, Patrisse Cullors, and Ayọ Tometi, became a movement. Coming back to the community organizers, creators, movers, and shakers, women started the movement.

The next panelist, Brittany Packnett, co-founder of Campaign Zero, formerly serving on the Ferguson Commission and President Obama's Task Force on 21st Century Policing, speaks about truth. I remember her opening: "Mothers should not have to go home to a dead child." That is a fact. But since this continues to happen, mothers should not have to fight alone. She sees the emotion that all of us are feeling and she challenges us, asking the question "What will your tears become?" It's a good and valid question, because without subsequent action our tears are useless. They mean nothing at all.

She goes on to suggest that oppression limits our imaginations. It stops us from thinking that radical change is possible. This is not the case—nor should it ever be. I think about everything else that can come out of our oppression. Our grandmothers faced the oppression head-on, often in strong and dignified silence, but our mothers are moving, shifting, and doing. They are encouraging us to use our voices and, if we need to, to scream. I think of Mamie Till, mother of fourteen-year-old Emmett—still a baby when they committed their unspeakable evil against him—and her insistence that the casket at his funeral be left open, because in her words, "I wanted the world to see what they did to my baby."[1] I think of her entire lifetime of community organizing, activism, and resilience that followed. I think of how she changed the world.

Then, I think of Victoire and her cooking, my own mother and her PhD at the age of fifty with three children at home. In the face of oppression we bring creativity, hopefulness, skill, talent, and verve. We bring grit. We bring resistance. We choose to resist by bringing all that we have. We go back so that we can move beyond.

Sybrina Fulton, the mother of Trayvon Martin, steps up to take the floor. She tells us that she stays motivated by telling herself that she is strong. She repeats it over and over, and I do so with her: *I am strong, I am strong, I am strong.* She shares that as soon as she tells herself that she is strong, she starts to believe it and is able to pick herself up from crying on the floor. I feel in my stomach the truth of what she is saying. It is impossibly moving. We can speak out and declare whatever we want to be. We can speak it into existence. You tell yourself what you will become. She tells us that the other thing that is important to her is her son, and that not even his death can separate her from her love for him. And what does that love look like now? It looks like the possibility of helping someone else. The possibility of saving someone else's son keeps her from going under.

I sit with all this, reflecting on the mothers—all those who are turning their own pain into positive change. The world is a better place because they are in it. And yet, there is still a place—and an important one at that—for a real reckoning around the mental health and well-being of Black women. I sometimes mentally take myself all the way up the chain of Black women providing a listening ear to those who need to talk about their problems, or fighting to ensure that no other mother receives the call to say that her baby won't be coming home. I wonder to myself, Well, what happens right at the end? What happens to the person who carries the weight of a line of hardship? Who is listening to her offload? What happens to the woman who fights with every last inch of energy she has to bring justice to her daughter? Who is the person fighting to bring justice to her? We currently exist in a world where Black women carry more, and that is no longer (has never been) good enough. Our ancestors held the weight of an entire generation. Will we one day inherit that load? How do we squeeze enough sweetness from the bitterness in front of us so that our daughters won't arrive on this earth already thirsty?

According to recent research from the Joint Committee on Human Rights, Black women in the United States are three to five times more likely to die in childbirth than white women. According to the Centers for Disease Control and

Prevention, not only are they more likely to die bringing new life into the world but they are more likely to experience *preventable* maternal death compared to white women. Little research has been done into why this is, but what we do know is that Black women are not simply more predisposed to dying than white women. Rather, according to women who have survived—and the relatives of those who haven't—Black women are simply not listened to or believed when they say that they are in pain. They are not taken seriously when they report reduced fetal movements or declare their desire not to be forced into a rushed cesarean section. Life-threatening conditions such as preeclampsia go undiagnosed. Pregnant Black women arrive at hospitals eight centimeters dilated and ready to push because midwives, nurses, and doctors didn't believe them when they said that they were deep in labor. Even Serena Williams, winner of more Grand Slam singles than any tennis player in the Open Era, came out in 2018 to discuss how she almost died giving birth to her daughter. Although she articulated her fear that her shortness of breath could be a sign of what did in fact turn out to be a pulmonary embolism, Williams's valid concerns were met with the suggestion that her pain medication "might be making her confused."[2]

The alarming mortality rates and disturbing treatment of Black mothers in the UK are not much better. In 2021, the UK's National Institute for Health and Care Excellence (NICE) published guidance recommending that Black women with uncomplicated pregnancies be induced at thirty-eight weeks in what I can only assume with the most generous of feelings is a misguided attempt to do something about the statistics highlighting their increased risk of maternal mortality. Rather than addressing the structural issues behind the statistic and seeking to understand *why* this is the case, NICE put the onus on Black women to give birth earlier. Can we just let that sink in for a moment? And in case anyone was wondering, the guidance for white women with uncomplicated pregnancies remains at forty-one weeks. Doctors, birth campaigners, and activists have come out in their numbers to declare that these mass early inductions are not the answer to the very complicated circumstances surrounding the statistics. Furthermore, it once again strips agency and choice away from the Black women themselves, only aggravating an already increasingly worrying situation where Black women feel pressured into early inductions or medical procedures.

Looking even closer, the horrifying statistics that Black women are three to five times more likely to die in childbirth tell only one part of the story. For every woman who dies, around one hundred more suffer a serious or life-threatening complication during pregnancy, childbirth, or shortly after. In medical terms these are defined as the "near misses." There still is no data collected on this, with the excuse being that it is very difficult to define precisely what a "near miss" looks like. According to one study, Black women are 83 percent more likely to suffer a "near miss" than their white counterparts.[3] Terrifying. These are not isolated incidents. There is an emerging pattern of otherwise entirely healthy Black women being taken out in their prime—and their babies with them. We need to start speaking about this.

Some have tried to attribute the shocking mortality statistics to socioeconomic factors, but according to the Centers for Disease Prevention and Control the statistics regarding Black women's heightened risk of pregnancy-related death span income and education levels. The more likely reason then is nothing to do with the socioeconomic but rather that Black women, universally, are not listened to when they speak, something that is only compounded by proposed measures such as blanket inductions determined entirely on the basis of race. Historically, advancements in the field of gynecology were actually made by experiments tested—violently—on Black women, who, as the general consensus went, did not feel pain. We, as a society, need to grapple with the weight of this truth. We need to speak about motherhood in the context of both its sweet scent of hope and possibility and the fact that when it comes to Blackness they don't believe us when we tell them we are bleeding. Black women are literally bleeding to death in hospital beds as they bring new life into the world because they are seen as *strong* before they are seen as *human*.

This is even harder to comprehend when you consider that these numbers are actually worse for Black women living in Western countries. We do not see these same poor outcomes for those in Africa and the Caribbean, so any attempt at explaining these statistics away with a genetic theory are simply not true. The cause is systemic racism. We need to call it what it is.

In 2018, a community of professional birth workers and educators joined together to form SisterWeb, a community doula organization founded to address these inequities by offering community doula care at no cost to Black, Native Hawaiian, Pacific Islander, and Latinx pregnant people in San Francisco. Since then they have supported hundreds of new mothers through their journeys, empowering them with knowledge and resilience and working to dismantle the systemic healthcare limitations that have shut Black women out. And at the same time, this organization is restoring joy in the birthing process. They give space to global majority women's words, strengthening community-led networks of resilience and ensuring that even if the powers that be won't listen, they are taking matters into their own hands.

I return again, quietly pensive now, to this thread of gold. Woven into the tapestry of motherhood are mothers who have known greater pain than most can ever conceive of. Mothers who have known loss. Mothers who lost before they had their baby. Mothers who long to become. Motherhood is not an exclusive club. It welcomes in anyone who knows its joy, but also anyone who tastes its pain.

Reflecting on this, I again come back to the idea of the recipe for lemonade: taking a half-pint of water and using it to change—or save—a life. Black women—our foremothers;

the Sybrinas, the Genevas, the Mamies, the Valeries, and the Gwens—are taking their darkest moments and weaving them into light. What might my own recipe look like?

Channeling all that I learned in my aunt Eseen's kitchen, I get to work.

A recipe for resilience, or perhaps for healing:

STEP ONE:

Take a half-pint of healthy boundaries.

Start from a place of knowing what you will accept, what works for you. Know when to say no. Resilience has limits.

STEP TWO:

Add a cup of authenticity. Have a coherent philosophy for your life. Dare to hold true to it, and trust that eventually you will be respected because of, not in spite of, it. You are uniquely, joyfully complete.

STEP THREE:

Stir in some openness, some flexibility. Your opinions matter— they are yours, but know that circumstances can shift them; make room for change.

STEP FOUR:

Bake in a healthy dose of self-appreciation. Treasure your inherent beauty, outside and in—you are enough as you are.

STEP FIVE:

Cool with the knowledge of your purpose. Resilience is a thousand small steps, not one big one. Incremental movement, day by day. You are a single thread in the tapestry, woven from purest gold.

Chapter Ten

DAUGHTER

I WOKE UP THIS MORNING in a world where women in America have fewer rights than a gun. Than a piece of metal designed solely to wreak havoc, destruction, and death on anyone unfortunate enough to cross its path.

But we are women. We are *Black* women. We are daughters of the women they tried to burn, daughters of the women who crawled across burning coals, emptied themselves of all of their feelings, divested themselves of their vestments, withstood hatred, abuse, the emotional wasteland of being a nothing, a no one, a stereotype. So today, on the day that I woke up and realized that women in America have fewer rights than a gun, is the day that I dare to speak up and out and back.

These desperate, dark moments need all of us—every single thing that we can possibly bring to face these times ahead;

our fear, yes, but also our bravery. Every little piece of us. It is all valid. It is all needed.

We are the gutsy hope of our grandmothers, the daring dream of our daughters. We hold safe in our hands this thread of gold.

This is a letter to the daughter I hope I will one day have. It is a letter to her daughter. It is a letter to every single woman who will come after me. And it is infused with the fire of my mother, my grandmother, and the furious, glorious women who came before, standing for our rights—for anything but this.

To my daughter,

I wish you a life of glorious, mutinous simplicity.

I wish for you a bike with three wheels that you wobble and ride, the gap in your teeth and the wind in your 'fro, your own brand of special. Your signature, shall we say, as you ride not a bike but a chariot, queen of a world where simplicity rules. Where kindness prevails and possibility fuels you because nothing is off-limits—you would never consider it so. And you don't.

You pedal furiously into class and sit up straight as you learn, curious with your questions and dedicated with your task of finding out why flowers of all colors bloom from buds that are green and how the letters from the alphabet join together to write your name. Your own name; the beauty of that. I hope that you wear it like a badge of honor, that you will say it with pride as the spidery letters flow into joined-up handwriting and the day that you are allowed to use a pen for the first time. And use it you will as you write letters and notes and stories—writing your world in the mud and the sand, crafting playdates and sleepovers.

And soon you won't need that third wheel anymore as your chariot flies without support.

But never fear;

I am here.

If you need me,

If you fall,

I'll be there.

That's what my dad said when I learned to ride my two-wheeler bike and he turned to me and told me, "You don't need your daddy anymore."

"But, Daddy," I told him, confused at his reasoning, ready to put him right.

"But, Daddy, I do when I fall.""

My daughter, I hope you fly high for eternity but I promise you this: It is okay if you fall. Do not worry even when your heart breaks and you think you may never be whole again.

Because you will.

And you might cry,

---

* Word for word a true story.

but that's okay, because crying is allowed for you, my daughter.

I wish for you tears of joy when you get on an airplane for the first time alone, seeing worlds that so far were nothing more than a dream.

And that when you see them something in you clicks and connects—this is part of your becoming

(a wise woman once said).

And you bring this becoming home with you to a summer of sweaty exhilarating parties and nightclubs using your older cousin's ID.

And when your exam results come in you might cry again, because you put every piece of your heart into them—or maybe you didn't.

Doesn't matter. The world is yours now.

And you are leaving home with nothing but a notepad and a backpack and a heart full of stars.

To places where learning happens—the kind you find in books that open your mind but also the kind you find in not enough sleep and friends that you meet
    by chance
    and from the moment you look at each other you know that this is a soulmate best mate 'til death do us part kind of thing.

    You'll laugh till you cry
    and cry when life comes around hard—
    and it might.

It may hit you.

And, my daughter, it may hurt

but I wish for you that it will never hit you harder than you can withstand

and that one day you will look back on those moments, take a deep breath

breathe out the sorrow

breathe in the light of a you that feels right.

Just putting some time in front of it

helps a lot,

my daughter.

I wish for you love that holds you to account and holds you to the light and holds you when you're breaking

even if you don't know how to articulate it.

I pray that you learn how to articulate it.

I pray that you will never need to hold your voice or suppress yourself for fear of being "too much."

You could never be too much, my daughter, and I pray that in these magical, messy years of becoming that you don't work too hard

that you remember to see the sunsets

and sleep

and sometimes to say no.

Sometimes it is good to say no.

I wish for you good hair, good food, good conversations,

the kind that make your mind feel like it is growing
so large it might just implode

because you had never considered thinking in that
way before

and I wish for you that you can walk into any workplace you choose

with your head held high and your hair higher because you exude professional

no matter what you look like

and everybody knows that they are lucky to
have you.

You have nothing to prove.

You will never have anything to prove.

You are enough.

I wish you sunsets, late nights,

good coffee, long runs,

defending yourself when you know you're right,

saying sorry when you know you're wrong,

meeting new people,

staying home, staying in,

concerts, art exhibitions, football games,

not getting out of bed all day.

I wish you the freedom and the bravery to dare
to try

whatever it is that you like

without knowing how it will work out

or even caring

and feeling good in yourself in your body
with wealth
in more ways than money—
it's a generational thing.
I wish for you a foundation that you can build
up from
and that your grandmother will stand in your
golden
tower and look out in silent joyful amazement
weeping
for the sights that she never saw
whilst she was down in the basement
building brick by brick
her faint hope that one day you and I might see
the sky
and the light
and the sun rise from these heights
and when we lay her body to rest
I hope you remember that she was weary
from all the work with no reward
but then remember that there was a reward and the
reward was you.
Death is silence
and silence scares you
but silence can be golden
we can be peaceful
we don't have to be interrupted

we do not always have to be interrupted.

. . .

But I interrupt you today because I want you to
know, my daughter, that even if the world shows you
hostility
    doesn't align with my plan
    still hasn't recognized your beauty your worth
    more than any gun
    or legislation
    or politics over your precious life.
    Well guess what?
    It does not matter because what connects us,
    my daughter,
    will outlast their politics and their lawmaking and
their life taking.
    We can take, too.
    I want you to take
    take this thread of gold that ties you to me and me
to your grandmother who weaves pure silk as she sits
with your great-grandmother and your great-great-
grandmother.

And Malinda Russell, Michaela Coel, Mary McLeod
Bethune, and Breonna Taylor, Nina Simone, Hattie
McDaniel, Phillis Wheatley Peters, Wangari Maathai,
ad infinitum.

These women are in you right now

so how can anyone tell you that you are not destined for greatness?

You are greatness.

It is yours, my darling,

and these are the things I wish for you,

nothing much

just the usual

glorious, mutinous simplicity.

That is my wish for you, my daughter.

RETURN OF THE TIDE

I WONDER WHAT CHIARA VIGO thinks of as she dives down to the bottom of the seabed each spring. I wonder if she looks up to where the sunlight catches the waves in tantalizing ripples, a reminder of the world waiting just above the surface, just out of reach. I wonder if she basks in the silence of the world under the sea. Is this world a sacred one, removed from the noise and the chaos of life up there? Or is she eager to return to land, thinking of her mission: to preserve the secret of womankind and deliver it to generations still to come, generations still unknown, unheard of? Does she float in the sparkling azure sea, freed from any pain? Is she weightless in that water?

I imagine her to be weightless; the very process of retrieving the sea silk and beginning the weaving of what will one day be a vivid, exuberant tapestry loosening the shackles that hold her.

I love my Blackness. I love my hair, my food, my music, the brotherhood, sisterhood, family, and community. I love being part of something that came way before me and will be continued long after I have taken my last breath. I love the feeling that a space has been made for me and that I might make one for someone else. Most of all, though, I love the legacy that has been left; stories just waiting to be uncovered by anyone who takes the time to look. The excavation, the uncovering; the delicate crafting of this book, honoring lives this world owes so much to, is both a source of pride and an exercise in consciousness raising. We must stand united in our mission to lift these women's names out of obscurity, to herald them for their achievements and contributions. This is just the start of the unveiling of Black women's stories and lives and the heady, exhilarating, resilient threads of gold that we each bring to our shared tapestry. In every possible way, our strength is in our unity. We are weaving this together and the growing tapestry, though it will never be finished, is an incendiary call to arms, an exhibition of a collective resistance that rises together across countless differences. Let us hang it somewhere prominent and think on it when we next opt for silence, find our elephants, declare that we are enough, or even quite simply say *no*. Let us remember that we are as connected to a rich historical legacy as we are to the rapidly unfolding new narrative.

This thread of gold that ties me to my mother, my grand-mother, and the women who came before looks a lot like the color purple. Like the purple hibiscus as it opens, entering a space that's never been seen before. It is yellow as the fruit of the lemon, yellow as the bus that we shall not be moved from, yellow as the lemonade that we make as we take one pint of water and half of a yellow sun and transform the sour into something sustaining. It is red as the umbilical cord that once physically held us, and red like the blood that we bleed. It is green like the gardens of our mothers that we are still in search of and black like the flags that we wave as we frown, buckle down, and plant: bending as we sow, reaching as we climb. It is brown as the soil left down on the ground from the trees that we lift, leaving space for the seedlings to reach to the sun and to grow and to glow as they bask in its light. Golden. Gold. This thread of gold that ties me to my mother, my grandmother, and the women who came before looks a lot like the color purple.

And now, I guess, it looks a lot like me—like us. We are this thread of gold. Long may we shine.

ACKNOWLEDGMENTS

Thank you to Emi and to Phoebe for making a dream come true in bringing *This Thread of Gold* to America, in so many ways the heart of the tapestry. Thank you to Sharmaine for believing and seeing. Thank you to Karolina, Gordon, and Meredith for taking the baton at the many stages of the race and for flying. Thank you to Sophie, without whom I would never have known. Thank you to Kitty for sharing "Sea Silk" with me. Thank you to Gugu for bringing "Daughter" to animated life. Thank you to the entire team at Tiny Reparations Books for making this shine.

Thank you to Angus and to Jude, for generous love.

Thank you to my dad and "Queenie," my mama. I owe you everything.

To Ena, my nan, our matriarch. Because of you, I am. Because of you, I will become.

ACKNOWLEDGMENTS

To my sisters–soulmates–best mates, Laura and Hannah, thank you for being there for every single right move/wrong move/tentative, daring, hopeful step.

And finally, to "grandmother, the alchemist"—and the lineage of women who came before. To my "daughter," my mutinous dream of an alternative future—and the generations of women who will come after. This is for you.

NOTES

EPIGRAPHS

1. Alice Walker, *In Search of Our Mothers' Gardens* (San Diego: Harcourt Brace Jovanovich, 1983).
2. Bernardine Evaristo, *Girl, Woman, Other* (London: Hamish Hamilton, 2019).

PROLOGUE: CALL OF THE TIDE

1. You can listen to Kitty's song "Sea Silk" on YouTube here: https://www.youtube.com/watch?v=K7nlqNy6UEo.
2. Rita Fuller-Yates, "Harriet Powers (1837–1910)," Black Past, November 9, 2020, https://www.blackpast.org/african -american-history/harriet-powers-1837-1910.
3. Lucine Finch, "A Sermon in Patchwork," *Outlook* (October 1914).

CHAPTER ONE: SILENCE

1. Adam Gabbatt, "Aunt Jemima Brand to Change Name and Logo Due to Racial Stereotyping," *The Guardian* (June 17, 2020), https://www.theguardian.com/us-news/2020/jun/17/aunt-jemima-products-change-name-image-racial-stereotype.
2. Kate Rushin, *The Black Back-ups* (Ithaca, NY: Firebrand Books, 1993).
3. Katherine Nagasawa, "The Fight to Commemorate Nancy Green, the Woman Who Played the Original 'Aunt Jemima,'" NPR (June 19, 2020), https://www.wbur.org/npr/880918717/the-fight-to-commemorate-nancy-green-the-woman-who-played-the-original-aunt-jemi.
4. Nagasawa, "The Fight to Commemorate Nancy Green."
5. "Titanium" by Giorgio Tuinfort/David Guetta/Sia Furler/Nick Van De Wall; lyrics © Sony/ATV Songs LLC, What A Publishing Limited, EMI Music Publishing Ltd.
6. Michaela Coel, *Misfits: A Personal Manifesto* (London: Ebury Press, 2021).

CHAPTER TWO: DEFIANCE

1. Stephan Lesher, "The Short, Unhappy Life of Black Presidential Politics, 1972," *The New York Times* (June 25, 1972), https://www.nytimes.com/1972/06/25/archives/the-short-unhappy-life-of-black-presidential-politics-1972-black.html.
2. Rajini Vaidyanathan, "Before Hillary Clinton, There Was Shirley Chisholm," BBC News (January 26, 2016), https://www.bbc.co.uk/news/magazine-35057641.

3. Debra Michals, PhD, "Shirley Chisholm (1924–2005)," National Women's History Museum (2015), https://www .womenshistory.org/education-resources/biographies/shirley -chisholm.

4. "Shirley Chisholm," A Seat at the Table Exhibit, Edward M. Kennedy Institute for the United States Senate, https://www .bringyourownchair.org/about-shirley-chisholm.

5. Rowena Mason, "Diane Abbott: Misogyny and Abuse Are Putting Women off Politics," *The Guardian* (February 14, 2017), https://www.theguardian.com/politics/2017/feb/14 /diane-abbott-misogyny-and-abuse-are-putting-women-off -politics.

6. Gaby Hinsliff, "Diane Abbott May Be Flawed. But This Is Bullying," *The Guardian* (June 6, 2017), https://www .theguardian.com/commentisfree/2017/jun/06/diane-abbott -bullying-shadow-home-secretary-attacks.

7. Eleanor (@eleanorkpenny) "WHEN YOU COME AT THE QUEEN YOU BEST NOT MISS #GE2017," Twitter photo (June 9, 2017), https://twitter.com/eleanorkpenny/status /873003322827051009?s=20&t=TRFS3SLskxvQkN3qj CDNxw.

8. Nadine White, "'Even Strong Black Women Cry,' Diane Abbott Tells Supporters," *The Voice* (June 25, 2017), https://archive.voice-online.co.uk/article/even-strong-black -women-cry-diane-abbott-tells-supporters.

9. Aamna Mohdin, "Meghan Could Help Black Women Shed Harmful 'Strong' Trope, Says Diane Abbott," *The Guardian* (March 9, 2021), https://www.theguardian.com/uk-news /2021/mar/09/meghan-interview-could-help-black-women -shed-harmful-strong-trope-says-diane-abbott.

10. Sarah Marsh, "'We've All Done It': Diane Abbott Backed After Apology for Train Mojito," *The Guardian* (April 20, 2019), https://www.theguardian.com/politics/2019/apr/20/diane-abbott-apologises-for-drinking-mojito-on-public-transport.

11. Guilaine Kinouani, *Living While Black: The Essential Guide to Overcoming Racial Trauma* (London: Ebury Press, 2021).

12. Ella Lee, "Fact Check: Post Online about Georgia Gov. Brian Kemp's 2018 Win Is Partly False," *USA Today* (November 18, 2020), https://eu.usatoday.com/story/news/factcheck/2020/11/18/fact-check-partly-false-claim-gov-brian-kemp-and-2018-election/6327447002.

13. Alexis Okeowo, "Can Stacey Abrams Save American Democracy?," *Vogue* (August 12, 2019), https://www.vogue.com/article/stacey-abrams-american-democracy-vogue-september-2019-issue.

14. Michelle Ruiz, "How Stacey Abrams Is Turning the Tide in Georgia," *Vogue* (November 5, 2020), https://www.vogue.com/article/stacey-abrams-georgia-vote-turning-the-tide.

15. Lauren Fedor, "Stacey Abrams: The Political Strategist Who Won Georgia," *Financial Times* (January 8, 2021), https://www.ft.com/content/8af50180-bbab-4595-a32b-fe9af205f1ce.

16. Chelsea Bailey, "Stacey Abrams: The Woman Behind Biden's Biggest Surprise," BBC News (November 9, 2020), https://www.bbc.co.uk/news/world-us-canada-54875344.

17. Jessica Stern, "This Is What Pride Looks Like: Miss Major and the Violence, Poverty, and Incarceration of Low-Income Transgender Women," *The Scholar & Feminist Online* (Fall 2011/Spring 2012), https://web.archive.org/web/20140904220636/http://sfonline.barnard.edu/a-new-queer

-agenda/this-is-what-pride-looks-like-miss-major-and-the
-violence-poverty-and-incarceration-of-low-income
-transgender-women/0.

CHAPTER THREE: REINVENTION

1. Chimamanda Ngozi Adichie, "The Danger of a Single Story," TEDGlobal video (July 2009), https://www.ted.com/talks /chimamanda_ngozi_adichie_the_danger_of_a_single_story /no-comments/transcript.
2. Al Young, "'I'd Rather Play a Maid Than Be One,'" *The New York Times* (October 15, 1989), https://www.nytimes.com /1989/10/15/books/id-rather-play-a-maid-than-be-one .html.
3. Adrienne Gaffney, "*Hollywood*: Who Was Hattie McDaniel, the First Black Oscar Winner Played by Queen Latifah?," *Elle* (May 3, 2020), https://www.elle.com/culture/movies-tv /a32349691/who-was-hattie-mcdaniel-hollywood/.
4. Hadley Hall Meares, "The Icon and the Outcast: Hattie McDaniel's Epic Double Life," *Vanity Fair* (April 26, 2021), https://www.vanityfair.com/hollywood/2021/04/hattie -mcdaniel-gone-with-the-wind-oscars-autobiography.
5. Meares, "The Icon and the Outcast."
6. Jennifer Schuessler, "The Long Battle over 'Gone With the Wind,'" *The New York Times* (June 14, 2020), https://www .nytimes.com/2020/06/14/movies/gone-with-the-wind -battle.html.
7. Schuessler, "The Long Battle over 'Gone With the Wind.'"
8. Leonard J. Leff, "'Gone With the Wind' and Hollywood's Racial Politics," *The Atlantic* (December 1999), https://www

.theatlantic.com/magazine/archive/1999/12/gone-with-the
-wind-and-hollywoods-racial-politics/377919.

9. Meares, "The Icon and the Outcast."

10. Jill Watts, *Hattie McDaniel: Black Ambition, White Hollywood*
(New York: Amistad, 2005).

11. John Vaudry, "Hattie McDaniel: Guilty of Accepting
Stereotyped Roles or Pioneer Helping African-Americans Get
a Foot in Hollywood's Door?," *Pembroke Observer* (March 8,
2020), https://www.pembrokeobserver.com/opinion
/columnists/hattie-mcdaniel-guilty-of-accepting-stereotyped
-roles-or-pioneer-helping-afrian-americans-get-a-foot-in
-hollywoods-doorr.

12. Watts, *Hattie McDaniel*, 176.

13. Watts, *Hattie McDaniel*, 177.

14. Oscars, "Hattie McDaniel's Winning Best Supporting Actress:
12th Oscars (1940)," YouTube video (September 27, 2011),
https://www.youtube.com/watch?v=e7t4pTNZshA&t=5s.

15. Watts, *Hattie McDaniel*, 180.

16. Hattie McDaniel, "Hattie McDaniel Defies Critics in 1947
Essay: 'I Have Never Apologized,'" *The Hollywood Reporter*
(1947, reposted on February 19, 2015), https://www
.hollywoodreporter.com/movies/movie-news/hattie
-mcdaniel-defies-critics-1947-774493.

17. McDaniel, "Hattie McDaniel Defies Critics in 1947 Essay: 'I
Have Never Apologized.'"

18. Robert Beatty, "Where Is Hattie McDaniel's Oscar?," *South
Florida Times* (June 2, 2010), https://www.sfltimes.com
/uncategorized/where-is-hattie-mcdaniels-oscar.

19. Seth Abramovitch, "Oscar's First Black Winner Accepted Her
Honor in a Segregated 'No Blacks' Hotel in L.A.," *The*

Hollywood Reporter (February 19, 2015), https://www
.hollywoodreporter.com/movies/movie-news/oscars-first
-black-winner-accepted-774335.

20. Victoria M. Massie, "The First Black Oscar Winner Fought Segregated Housing in Los Angeles—and Won," *Vox*, February 24, 2016, https://www.vox.com/2016/2/24 /11105204/hattie-mcdaniel-housing-oscars.

21. Abramovitch, "Oscar's First Black Winner."

22. McDaniel, "Hattie McDaniel Defies Critics in 1947 Essay: 'I Have Never Apologized.'"

23. Watts, *Hattie McDaniel*, 142.

CHAPTER FOUR: FORMATION

1. Lola Olufemi, "Celebrating the Radical, Revolutionary Life of Claudia Jones," *gal-dem* (September 24, 2021), https://gal-dem .com/celebrating-the-radical-revolutionary-life-of-claudia -jones.

2. Vertamae Smart-Grosvenor, *Vibration Cooking: or, the Travel Notes of a Geechee Girl* (New York: Doubleday, 1970).

3. Maryse Condé, *Victoire: My Mother's Mother* (New York: Atria Books, 2006).

4. T. Denean Sharpley-Whiting, "*Femme négritude:* Jane Nardal, *La Dépêche africaine*, and the Francophone New Negro," *Souls* (Fall 2000), Columbia University, http://www.columbia.edu /cu/ccbh/souls/vol2no4/vol2num4art1.pdf.

5. Dan Feldman, "LeBron James: Neighbor's Walls, Not Breonna Taylor, Got Justice," NBC Sports (September 24, 2020), https://nba.nbcsports.com/2020/09/24/lebron-james -neighbors-walls-not-breonna-taylor-got-justice/.

6. Ta-Nehisi Coates, "The Life Breonna Taylor Lived, in the Words of Her Mother," *Vanity Fair* (August 24, 2020), https://www.vanityfair.com/culture/2020/08/breonna-taylor.

7. "Formation" by Beyoncé Knowles/Michael Williams/Asheton Hogan/Khalif Brown; lyrics © WB Music Corp., Warner-Tamerlane Publishing Corp., Oakland 13 Music, Sounds From Eardrummers LLC, Eardrummers Entertainment LLC.

CHAPTER FIVE: WARRIOR

1. Audre Lorde, *A Burst of Light* (Ithaca, NY: Firebrand Books, 1988).

2. Isabelle Waterfall, "My Name Is Peaches: The Story of Nina Simone," *Bluestocking* (September 13, 2017), https://blue-stocking.org.uk/2017/09/13/my-name-is-peaches-the-story-of-nina-simone/.

3. W. E. B. Du Bois, *The Souls of Black Folk* (Chicago: A. C. McClurg & Co., 1903).

4. Waterfall, "My Name Is Peaches."

5. Sherrie Tucker, *Swing Shift: "All-Girl" Bands of the 1940s* (Durham, NC: Duke University Press, 2000).

CHAPTER SIX: QUEEN

1. DeNeen L. Brown, "Was Queen Charlotte Black?," *Seattle Times* (December 27, 2020), https://www.seattletimes.com/nation-world/was-queen-charlotte-black-heres-what-we-know/.

2. "Black" by Fraser T. Smith/David Omoregie; lyrics © Neighbourhood, Kobalt Music Publishing. The live

performance at the BRITs 2020 is worth watching if you haven't (and again and again if you have), https://www .youtube.com/watch?v=mXLS2IzZSdg.

3. Kingsley Ighobor, "Wangari Maathai, the Woman of Trees, Dies," African Renewal online, United Nations, https://www .un.org/africarenewal/web-features/wangari-maathai-woman -trees-dies.

4. Florynce R. Kennedy, *Color Me Flo: My Hard Life and Good Times* (Saddle River, NJ: Prentice Hall, 1976).

5. Hannah Militano, "Who Was Flo Kennedy? Learn All About the Fiery Black Feminist and Civil Rights Activist," *L'Officiel* (February 9, 2021), https://www.lofficielusa.com/politics -culture/who-was-florynce-flo-kennedy-black-feminist -activist.

6. Sherie M. Randolph, *Florynce "Flo" Kennedy: The Life of a Black Feminist Radical* (Chapel Hill: University of North Carolina Press, 2015).

7. Douglas Martin, "Flo Kennedy, Feminist, Civil Rights Advocate and Flamboyant Gadfly, Is Dead at 84," *The New York Times* (December 23, 2000), https://www.nytimes.com /2000/12/23/us/flo-kennedy-feminist-civil-rights-advocate -and-flamboyant-gadfly-is-dead-at-84.html.

8. Randolph, *Florynce "Flo" Kennedy.*

9. Azi Paybarah, "N.Y. Today: Black New Yorkers, Overlooked, Until Now," *The New York Times* (February 7, 2019), https:// www.nytimes.com/2019/02/07/nyregion/newyorktoday /ny-news-black-history.html.

10. "Gladys Bentley: A Gender-Bending Blues Performer, Who Became 1920s Harlem Royalty: Videos, Photos," *Jazz Blues News* (February 9, 2019), https://jazzbluesnews.com/2019

/02/09/gladys-bentley-a-gender-bending-blues-performer
-who-became-1920s-harlem-royalty-videos-photos.

11. Gladys Bentley, "I Am a Woman Again," *Ebony* (August 1952), https://www.digitaltransgenderarchive.net/files/xs55 mc356.

12. Una Marson, "Black Burden," *The Moth and the Stars* (Kingston, Jamaica: self-published, 1937).

CHAPTER SEVEN: PIONEER

1. I wrote in more detail about my experiences using wild swimming to heal from my grief in my article "How Wild Swimming as a Black Woman Helped Me Heal from My Grief," published on Refinery29 (September 28, 2021), https://www.refinery29.com/en-gb/wild-swimming-black -woman-mental-health.

2. Ashawnta Jackson, "How Mary Fields Became 'Stagecoach Mary,'" JSTOR Daily (March 19, 2021), https://daily.jstor .org/how-mary-fields-became-stagecoach-mary.

3. Natalie Morris, "FINA Apologises for Rejecting Inclusive Afro Hair Swim Cap from Olympics," *Metro* (July 21, 2021), https://metro.co.uk/2021/07/21/fina-apologises-for-inclusive -afro-hair-swim-cap-rejection-14963360.

4. Erica Richardson, MD, PhD, "The State of Mental Health of Black Women: Clinical Considerations," *Psychiatric Times* (September 23, 2021), https://www.psychiatrictimes.com /view/the-state-of-mental-health-of-black-women-clinical -considerations.

CHAPTER EIGHT: GRANDMOTHER

1. "All Night" by Akil King, André Benjamin, Antwan Patton, Beyoncé, Henry "Red" Allen, Ilsey Juber, Jaramye Daniels, Patrick Brown, Theron Thomas, Thomas Wesley Pentz, Timothy Thomas.
2. Taylor-Dior Rumble, "Claudette Colvin: The 15-Year-Old Who Came before Rosa Parks," BBC World Service (March 10, 2018), https://www.bbc.co.uk/news/stories-43171799.
3. Rumble, "Claudette Colvin."
4. Gary Younge, "She Would Not Be Moved," *The Guardian* (December 15, 2000), https://www.theguardian.com/theguardian/2000/dec/16/weekend7.weekend12.
5. Younge, "She Would Not Be Moved."
6. Younge, "She Would Not Be Moved."
7. Rumble, "Claudette Colvin."
8. Younge, "She Would Not Be Moved."
9. Younge, "She Would Not Be Moved."
10. Jo Stanley, "Women of Windrush: Britain's Adventurous Arrivals That History Forgot," *New Statesman* (June 22, 2018), https://www.newstatesman.com/politics/2018/06/women-windrush-britain-s-adventurous-arrivals-history-forgot.
11. Notting Hill Carnival History, https://nhcarnival.org/experience/history.
12. Charlotte Pierce-Baker, *Surviving the Silence: Black Women's Stories of Rape* (New York: W. W. Norton, 1998).
13. Pierce-Baker, *Surviving the Silence.*
14. Brooke Axtell, "Black Women, Sexual Assault and the Art of Resistance," *Forbes* (April 25, 2012), https://www.forbes.com/sites/shenegotiates/2012/04/25/black-women-sexual-assault-and-the-art-of-resistance.

15. Tobi Thomas, "Beverley Bryan: The British Black Panther Who Inspired a Generation of Women," *The Guardian* (January 28, 2021), https://www.theguardian.com/society /2021/jan/28/beverley-bryan-the-british-black-panther-who -inspired-a-generation-of-women.

16. Thomas, "Beverley Bryan."

17. Thomas, "Beverley Bryan."

18. Thomas, "Beverley Bryan."

CHAPTER NINE: MOTHER

1. DeNeen L. Brown, "Emmett Till's Mother Opened His Casket and Sparked the Civil Rights Movement," *The Washington Post* (July 12, 2018), https://www .washingtonpost.com/news/retropolis/wp/2018/07/12 /emmett-tills-mother-opened-his-casket-and-sparked-the -civil-rights-movement.

2. Amanda Randone, "Black Mothers Are Five Times More Likely to Die During Childbirth. That Needs to Change," *British Vogue* (July 25, 2020), https://www.vogue.co.uk /beauty/article/black-maternal-mortality.

3. "New Loughborough Research Will Use Artificial Intelligence to Help Reduce Maternal Harm amongst Mothers from Black Ethnic Groups," Loughborough University (November 17, 2021), https://www.lboro.ac.uk/departments/compsci /news/2021/new-research-help-reduce-maternal-harm.

INDEX

ABOUT THE AUTHOR

Catherine Joy White is an actor, writer, filmmaker, and founder and CEO of the award-winning Kusini Productions, a company established to champion the voices of Black women. She is a gender adviser to the United Nations, has been long-listed for AllBright's Innovative Trailblazer Award, and has been honored as a member of the *Forbes* 30 Under 30 Class of 2022. She starred in Amazon Prime Video's *Ten Percent*, the UK adaptation of *Call My Agent!*, and worked on the 2023 season of *Black Mirror* alongside Salma Hayek Pinault. Her films have been funded by the British Film Institute and the BBC, and have won awards at BAFTA- and Oscar-qualifying festivals worldwide. She wrote and directed *To My Daughter*, a film starring Gugu Mbatha-Raw, which was adapted from a chapter in *This Thread of Gold*. She has a master's degree in women's studies from the University of Oxford and an undergraduate degree from the University of Warwick. She lives in Oxford, and this is her debut book.